Collins

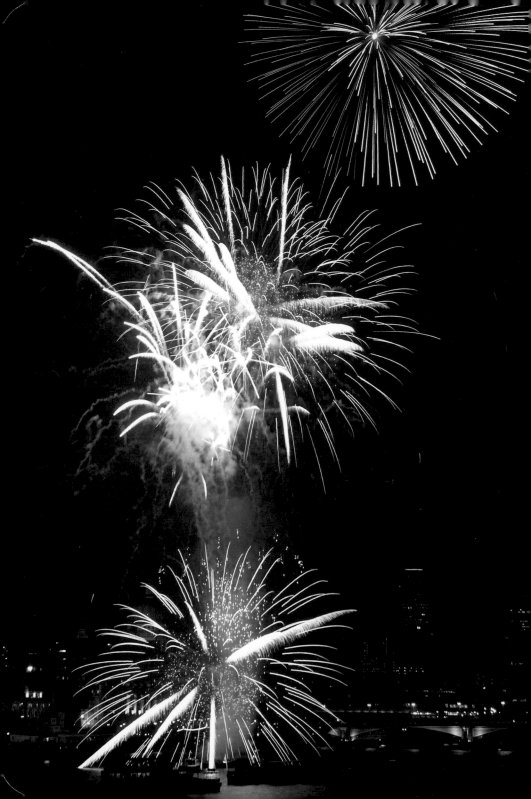

need to know?

Digital SLR
Photography

John Freeman

Collins

First published in 2008 by
Collins, an imprint of
HarperCollins Publishers
77–85 Fulham Palace Road
Hammersmith, London W6 8JB

The Collins website address is:
www.collins.co.uk

Collins is a registered trademark of HarperCollins Publishers Limited

12 11 10 09 08
6   5   4   3   2   1

A catalogue record for this book is available from the British Library.

Technical Contributor: **Doug Harman**
Created by: **SP Creative Design**
Editor: **Heather Thomas**
Designer: **Rolando Ugolini**

Photography
All photography by John Freeman
www.johnfreeman-photographer.com

Based on material from *Collins Digital SLR Handbook*

ISBN: 978-0-00-725939-7

Printed and bound by **Printing Express Ltd., Hong Kong**

Contents

Introduction

For many years now, the 35mm SLR film camera has been the cornerstone of the serious photographer's kit, but, with a speed that few people could have imagined, the digital single lens reflex (DSLR) camera has now taken over its role.

The rise of the DSLR

There are those people who still maintain that the age of digital photography is all about 'manipulation' and that photographs produced digitally cannot come close to those printed on bromide in a wet darkroom. While no one would deny that shooting on film, developing it and then making a print is a craft that one spends a lifetime learning, equally no one should underestimate the different skills required to get the best from a digital camera, especially a sophisticated DSLR model.

Digital developments

Since the mid-1970s, when Kodak developed the first solid-state image sensor, the developments in digital photography have been as varied as they have been rapid. Only a few years ago, for instance, a compact camera boasting a 2mp (megapixel) image sensor was thought of as state of the art.

Comparing that to, say, my Canon EOS 1DS MK2 DSLR, which has a 17mp image sensor, it would be foolish to think that the technology will do anything but improve. This camera has now become the centre of my kit, and there are few applications it cannot cope with just as well as, if not better than, my old film cameras once did.

The DSLR camera body is at the centre of a vast and continually growing system that is perfect for the professional photographer and enthusiastic amateur. Apart from being able to record high-definition images that can be enlarged to billboard-size proportions, the lenses available can be applied to virtually any shooting situation. Then there are the accessories, such as interchangeable focusing screens, macro ring flash, angle finders, underwater housings and so on. However, just as it was with the old film SLRs or any equipment, it is you, the photographer, who makes the difference. After all, it is your 'eye' that sees the picture – the camera can only record it in the way you tell it to. This book will help you to see in a way that will enable you to get the most from your DSLR system.

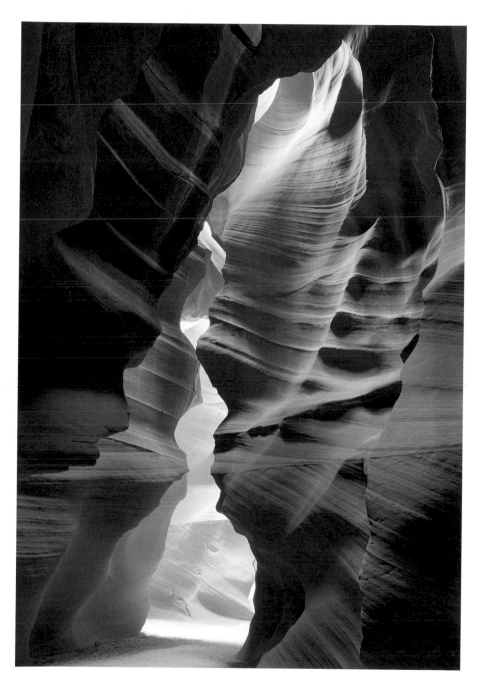

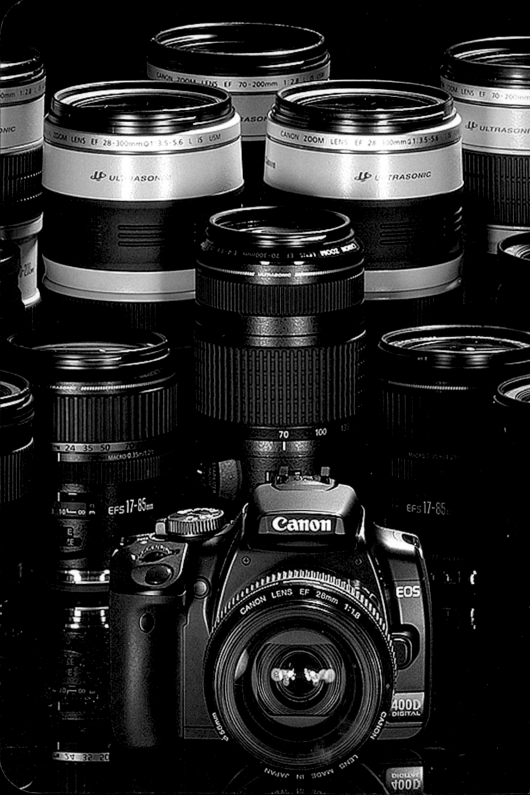

1 The DSLR system

Digital SLR cameras developed out of film SLRs. The earliest models were actually hybrids of film and digital technology but, as digital technology has advanced, DSLRs have become the camera of choice for many professional and amateur photographers. With its wide range of accessories, the DSLR can handle just about any shooting situation, and as the technology advances, with 'full frame' sensors now becoming the norm, the quality of large prints are beginning to surpass those produced in the 'wet darkroom'.

The DSLR explained

The main difference between a DSLR and an SLR camera is that in a DSLR, the film is replaced by a solid-state image sensor. The images are created digitally within the camera, without the need to develop an image on film using chemicals.

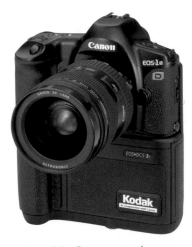

One of the first cameras that was produced by Kodak and Canon was the EOS DCS 3, comprising a Canon EOS 1N film body adapted to take a Kodak digital 'back'. The camera shows how the early digital SLRs were a hybrid of film and digital technology.

How it all started

In the mid-1970s, Kodak developed the first solid-state image sensor, known today as a CCD (charge coupled device), and by 1986, it had unveiled to the world the first megapixel sensor. With 1.4mp (megapixels), it was able to produce a photograph measuring around 130 x 170mm (5 x 7in). Kodak then moved on to develop the Photo CD system for digitizing and storing photographs on a CD.

It was fitting that, in 1991, Kodak revealed the first commercially available DCS (digital camera system). Aimed at professionals, its DCS 100 was made up of a Nikon F3 camera body and a Kodak digital camera back with a 1.3 megapixel sensor on board.

Advances in technology

The benefits afforded to digital photographers quickly became apparent as the technology proved itself. Admittedly, the cameras available were chunky and needed a bus for carting the batteries around on, and they were also expensive: some of the first DSLRs cost over £20,000, making them a serious investment for any professional snapper and out of the reach of most enthusiast photographers. However, the fact that you had a fast turnaround of images, could check your shot on the back of the camera as you went and had no film and development costs became key factors in the growing popularity of DSLRs. You could also use the same lenses on your digital SLR as on a film SLR, so owners of Canon and Nikon digital SLRs (the first two main manufacturers working with Kodak to make the digital aspects of the machines) did not need to buy lots of other kit.

Slowly, the move – for professionals at first, then for amateurs – from film to digital grew apace. The technology became (and continues to become) better and cheaper. And the key benefits of speed and control, plus the removal of worries over film and film processing, meant that any photojournalist who didn't swap over to digital would be left behind in the rush to get their images on the picture editor's desk.

The introduction of Nikon's D1, fully integrated and, for the first time, complete DSLR (not needing the addition of a digital 'back') in 1999 transformed the marketplace. At last, there was a complete, user-friendly, reasonably sized and, importantly, reasonably priced DSLR, and it took the market by storm. Well made and featuring all the photography tools you would expect from a top-end model but in a svelte package, the D1 left almost everyone wanting to own one. It also meant that there was no turning back for the marketplace.

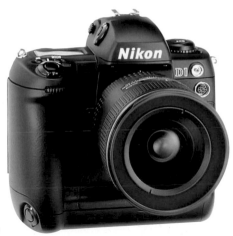

Nikon's ground-breaking DSLR, the D1, revolutionized not only the DSLR camera market, but also what photographers came to expect from their cameras.

The Canon EOS 400D marks the latest in the company's line of DSLRs aimed at the beginner end of the market, but still boasts a 10.1 megapixel sensor and a host of advanced features.

The range of DSLRs

Today's DSLRs cover a broad spectrum of the marketplace: there are cameras to suit everyone, from novice users, those swapping from film to digital, as well as high-end professionals.

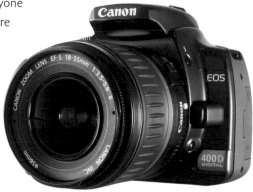

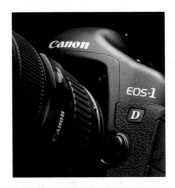

Canon's EOS 1D MK2 represents one of the high-end DSLRs designed for professional use. Even though the body is tougher and the internals more complex than those of less expensive EOS DSLRs, it can still use the same range of lenses and accessories.

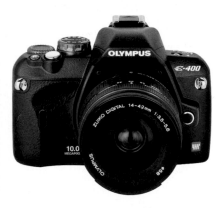

Olympus's E400 FourThirds system DSLR camera features a small, easy-to-use body and a Kodak-developed 4:3 aspect ratio sensor requiring a new lens mount and lenses. Its compact size is an advantage.

Those cameras aimed specifically at the novice, such as Canon's EOS 400D and Nikon's D50, are still extremely sophisticated pieces of kit but they are both built to a price. Consequently, they lack the professional level of build quality, some of the finer control available on most higher-end models and also some of the faster internal processors that make them tick.

Sony has entered the fray with its first DSLR, the Sony Alpha 100, based on Konica Minolta technology. Olympus has taken a different route, with Kodak (again), and developed a new range of DSLRs for the professional and enthusiast featuring the specially developed FourThirds system. This incorporates a range of new lenses and a new 4:3 aspect ratio Kodak sensor (hence the name of the system). Nikon, meanwhile, has introduced another enthusiast level DSLR in the shape of the D80.

At the top end of the DSLR scale, there are the professional-level DSLRs, which are typically built to withstand the knocks meted out on, say, match day at a football ground in the pouring rain, and the dust and dirt of harsh environments, such as war zones. The camera bodies and the internal electronics are tough, all of them offer high-resolution sensors capable of the highest image quality, and they come at a premium in price as well.

Advantages of DSLRs

DSLRs are extremely versatile, offering you key advantages over compact digital cameras and many SLRs. The fact that they can use a range of varying focal length lenses or lenses designed for specific tasks is, of course, key to their success.

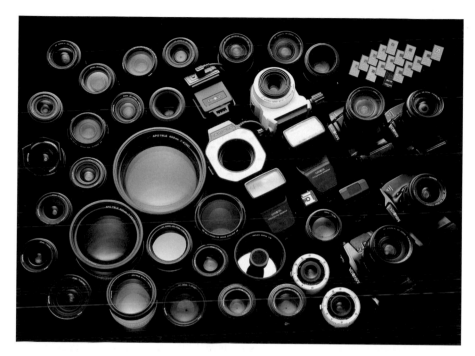

Since DSLRs come with larger lenses and brighter glass elements than those that are available to digital compacts, it means that they offer higher-resolution optics. The amount of detail that can be captured is increased and the wide range of optics available for a variety of jobs helps, too. With a DSLR, you can cater for all tasks, including specialist jobs, such as macro photography, where the lens must be able to focus very close to the subject, and architectural work, where a shift or tilt lens can correct converging verticals.

Accessories, such as flash guns that mount on a hotshoe on top of the camera allowing for more control of lighting, provide even more versatility, as does the ability to use studio flash systems for professional portrait shoots, for example.

A DSLR is part of a system of lenses and accessories that enables the photographer to shoot a huge variety of subjects while retaining complete control of the shoot, making this type of camera truly versatile.

The equipment

Foremost in any camera system is the camera body, followed by its lenses and the accessories that help to expand the capabilities of both; these include flash guns, lens filters, hoods and so on.

must know

Light information is passed from the sensor to the processor, which must chew on the data to get the most from the image, dealing with colour processing, image compression, and the colour display and white balance. Whatever the camera and processor's name, they all do the same jobs, helping make the most of your images.

Sensor

DSLRs use special, light-sensitive sensors to capture light and record images. There are three types of sensor: the CCD (charge coupled device), the CMOS chip (complementary metal oxide sensor) and the Foveon X3 sensor. They use millions of tiny, discrete picture elements, known as pixels. The more pixels there are, the higher the resolution. The CCD and CMOS chips have their pixels laid out on a flat plane, and each pixel can be thought of as a small light well.

Every pixel has a tiny micro lens on top of it that helps to focus the light properly within each pixel. Any light entering a pixel is converted to a digital signal and sent to the camera's on-board computer. The captured light is given a value corresponding to its brightness and colour, and all these values added together form the final digital image we see.

The actual quality of an image is dependent on not just the sensor but the entire DSLR system, such as the metering, white balance control, image processing and, most importantly, the lens. Poor-quality lenses deliver poor-quality light to the sensor, so the better the optics within a camera system, the better the images. No matter how many pixels a sensor houses and no matter how good the processor (see box), if the light is blurred as it hits the CCD, your pictures are compromised.

Viewfinder and pentaprism

The viewfinder allows you to see what you're about to shoot through the lens mounted on the camera. Top-end DSLRs have a field of view (the amount of the subject the lens will capture) that represents 100 per cent of the scene before you; less expensive models have around a 95 per cent field of view.

Shooting information is usually on show through the viewfinder, along with the number of exposures left on a memory card, the shutter speed and aperture in use and if flash is activated or needed.

The key to all this utility is the pentaprism: a five-sided reflecting prism that catches the light entering the lens, turns it over, then flips it back into the viewfinder for you to see, without inverting the image. Some lower-end DSLRs use a pentamirror set-up instead of a pentaprism. However, they are not so bright as pentaprism viewfinders, which makes viewing more difficult in low light.

lens   lens barrel   camera body   viewfinder

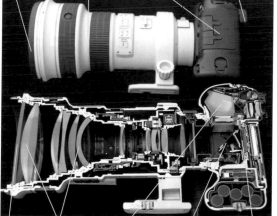

In this cutaway of a Canon EOS 1DS, the largest element is the lens on the front. The internal lenses and their curvatures show how light is captured, channelled down the lens barrel, focused and passed on, into the camera body. The light encounters a 45-degree angled mirror that directs it upwards through a pentaprism to the viewfinder.

front   internal lens   pentaprism   45-degree   sensor
lens   elements   angled mirror

Equipment care

A DSLR system represents a significant investment, so it pays to look after it, especially as repairing a piece of equipment after the warranty has expired could be extremely costly, sometimes amounting to even more than the purchase price.

Care and common sense

Caring for a DSLR and lenses is a matter of common sense. Do not drop them, and keep them free from dirt, dust, sand and water. Keep your camera and lenses in a well-padded camera bag when not in use. To clean externally, wipe the camera with a lint-free cloth – a microfibre lens cloth is ideal, as the tiny microfibres absorb dirt and finger grease.

When inserting memory cards or electrical leads, never use force, and always put them in the right way round. Rubber caps over external sockets must be tightly shut. If you store your DSLR for any length of time, place it in a camera bag with a pack of silica gel to reduce moisture levels. Remember to remove the batteries, which could leak and cause corrosion.

Protecting the sensor

Many DSLRs have sensors that are not shielded from dust, so each time you swap a lens, dust can fly in and perch on the sensor. To prevent this, try changing your lenses in a clean plastic bag and keep the camera shielded from draughts or wind when switching optics. If dust does get in, a small lens blower-bulb and a gentle puff of air on the sensor might help. Try this with the camera facing down, and all but the most stubborn dirt should drop out.

Lenses

The DSLR system comes with the widest range of different lenses available to cameras. Even medium-format cameras, such as Hasselblads, and large-format models and rangefinder types, such as Leicas, have far fewer compatible lenses.

Range of lenses

Not only are DSLR lenses available in different focal lengths, from fisheye to ultra telephoto, but there are also many specialist lenses, such as shift and tilt lenses and macro lenses. (See pages 18-21 for pictures of the most usual lenses and the types of image that they produce.) In addition to the lenses made by the camera manufacturers, there are also many independent lens producers who supply competitively priced alternatives.

With such an array, you might feel daunted trying to select suitable lenses. What's important is that you buy the best in their field – there is no substitute for high-precision optics. If that seems extravagant, remember that your lenses will outlast your camera by years, provided they are treated with care.

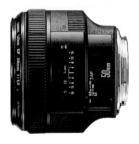

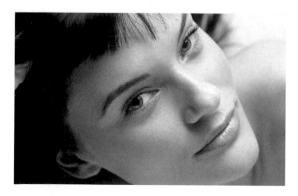

50mm focal length lenses, when used with the 35mm format, have roughly the same field of view as the human eye, which makes them perfect for recording images in much the same way as when we first see them, with little distortion or compression.
> Canon EOS 1DS, 50mm lens, 1/125 sec, f/8.

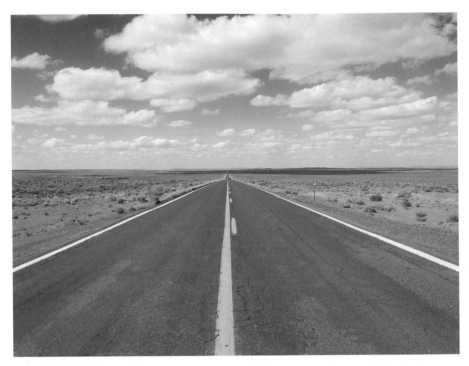

Wide-angle lenses, such as 24mm, are perfect for shooting expansive landscapes. However, it is all too easy to include great swathes of uninteresting detail in foregrounds and bland skies. In this shot, the road and cloud detail add to the composition.
> Canon EOS 1DS, 24mm lens, 1/400 sec, f/11.

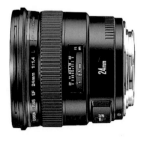

Buying lenses

When I buy a lens, it's because I need it for a specific purpose and because I know I will get the maximum use out of it. Although it might be desirable to have a 600mm telephoto lens in my kit, the financial outlay cannot be justified – lenses such as this cost thousands – unless I am going to do a lot of wildlife or sports photography, for example. If I intended to use it only occasionally, I would consider hiring one from a professional photographic dealer instead.

Three lenses form the cornerstone of my kit: these are 16-35mm, 24-70mm and 70-200mm lenses. With these I have wide-angle, normal and telephoto capabilities that cover most shooting situations. They all have a maximum wide aperture of f/2.8 throughout their range (see below), and their quality is superb. Because I tend to shoot a lot of architectural subjects, I have a range of shift and tilt lenses, which are invaluable for correcting converging verticals. I also have a fisheye lens, which is particularly useful when shooting interiors of large buildings, such as churches. A macro lens completes the kit – I use this for close-up work, chiefly nature subjects.

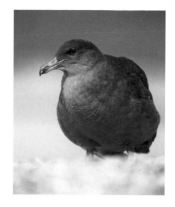

Telephoto lenses are great for bringing distant subjects closer. This is essential in photographing wildlife, where being near to the subject might scare it away.
> Canon EOS 1DS MK2, 200mm lens, 1/500 sec, f/2.8.

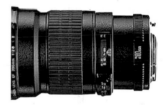

Apertures

All lenses have a maximum aperture, such as f/1.4, f/2.8 or f/5.6. Those lenses with a maximum wide aperture of f/1.4 are sometimes referred to as 'faster' than a lens of the same focal length whose maximum aperture is f/5.6. The quality of a fast lens is far superior to that of a slower one.

The maximum aperture on a zoom lens can vary. For instance, a 70–200mm lens might have a maximum aperture of f/3.5 when it is set at 70mm, but the maximum aperture might be only f/5.6 when set at 200mm. This loss of speed might create problems if you are shooting in low light.

In my experience, a zoom lens with a variable aperture will not have the resolving power and sharpness of a lens that has a constant aperture throughout its focal length range, such as f/2.8. However, you might end up paying up to four times more for this superiority in a lens. Wider-angle lenses, due to their inherent characteristics, have greater maximum apertures than telephotos, such as f/2.8, while a superior 600mm telephoto might have a maximum aperture of only f/4. However, for a 600mm lens this is extremely fast.

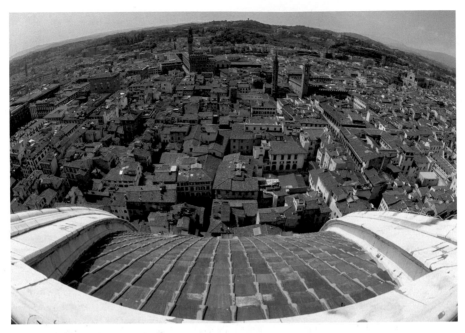

Fisheye lenses have limited uses, but they can create eye-catching shots, often giving a different outlook on familiar views, such as the cityscape of Florence (above). The 180° view of a fisheye means you need to be extra careful about what you include in the frame.
> Canon EOS 1DS, 15mm f/2.8 fisheye lens, 1/250 sec, f/8.

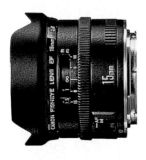

Sensor size

At the top end of the DSLR range, most lenses have sensors equivalent in size to the old 35mm format (i.e. 24 x 36mm), which means they are compatible to the focal lengths attributed to them. However, many DSLRs come with a sensor too small to capture the same image possible with a film camera. This is not a problem when taking portraits or if you need maximum telephoto capabilities, but it can be with wide-angle lenses. A 28mm lens on a DSLR with a sensor of only 23 x 15mm, say, will result in the lens having an equivalent focal length of only 44mm, which is hardly wide angle. Manufacturers are now producing ever wider lenses – whereas 17mm would have been thought of as extreme only a few years ago, you can now buy a wide-angle lens with a focal length of only 10mm for a DSLR camera.

Ghosting and flare

Another problem with DSLR lenses, particularly long lenses, is 'mirror' reflection. The sensors in digital cameras are different from their film equivalents and have a reflectivity that creates flare and ghosting inside the lens. For example, if you were to use a 300mm telephoto lens with a protective glass flat in front of the first lens element, any light that is entering the lens from a bright light source would be reflected off the sensor and back onto the protective glass, causing ghosting.

To eliminate this 'mirror' reflection problem, some DSLR camera manufacturers now make their

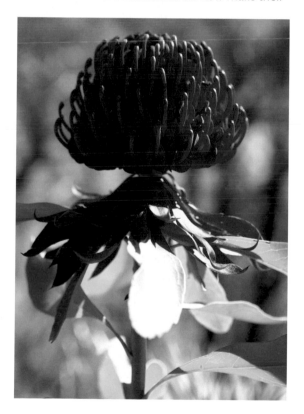

Macro lenses enable you to get close to nature (magnification up to life size is possible) and are excellent for photographing plants and flowers. Working distances can be problematic in some situations due to the proximity of the lens to the subject.
> Canon EOS 1DS, 100mm f/2.8 macro lens, 1/85 sec, f/5.6.

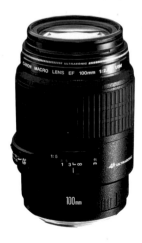

lenses with a meniscus lens (one convex and one concave side with equal curvatures) that is used in place of the flat protective glass. The meniscus lens means that the light reflected from the sensor forms an image in front of it and then disperses. As most light that is dispersed does not hit the reflective elements, the problems of ghosting and flare are thereby prevented.

Viewed from top to bottom and left to right, this sequence of views over the River Thames shows how different lenses capture the same scene from the same viewpoint.

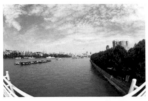

fisheye

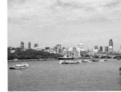

50mm

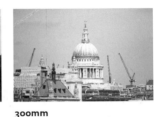

300mm

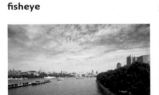

16mm

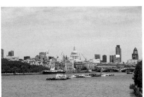

70mm

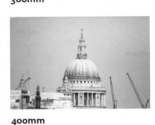

400mm

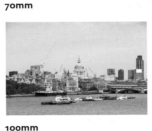

24mm

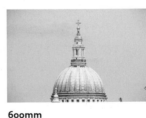

100mm

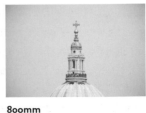

600mm

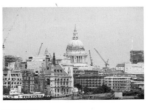

35mm

200mm

800mm

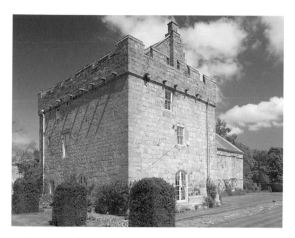

Shift and tilt lenses are among the specialist lenses available to the DSLR camera user. They are especially suited to architectural photography, as they eliminate the problem known as converging verticals, where buildings appear to taper towards the top.
> Canon EOS 1DS, 24mm f/3.5 TS-E lens, 1/400 sec, f/11.

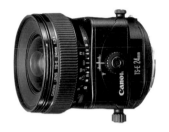

Fringing

What we perceive as white light is, in fact, a combination of different colours uniformly mixed, so that we do not see any one colour in particular. If we shine this light through a prism, it will disperse, creating a rainbow-type spectrum caused by refraction – this is because the individual colour wavelengths are focused at different points. To some extent, the same thing happens with our photographic lenses. Called 'chromatic aberration', it appears as 'fringing' along the edges of the subject matter in photographs.

In good-quality lenses, this is corrected by a combination of different types of optical glass with different dispersal and refraction qualities. In lens construction, these are known as 'elements' and are placed in the lens barrel in a series of 'groups'. It is this combination, together with the quality of the glass, its shape and coating, that makes one lens superior to another, even if it's the same focal length. This also explains why some lenses cost considerably more than others.

must know

Zoom lenses are a great way of reducing the amount of kit you need to carry. Three zoom lenses, such as a 16-35mm, 24-70mm and 70-200mm, will cover most normal situations. They are also good for creating in-camera effects.

Accessories

Having selected your lenses, there are several accessories that you should consider buying, not only to help you make the most of your camera and lenses but also to protect them.

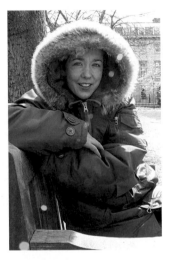

Without a lens hood, flare can enter the lens, as it has in this shot, ruining the photograph.

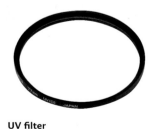

UV filter

UV and skylight filters

UV and skylight filters make virtually no difference to colour temperature and exposure, although the UV filter does absorb UV light without cutting visible light, reducing haze on sunny days, while a skylight filter reduces the blue cast caused by sky and water reflections. Despite such minimal effects, I have one of these filters permanently attached to my lenses to protect them from dust and scratches – after all, a filter costs only a few pounds, whereas a lens might cost thousands.

Lens hoods and shields

I always fit a lens hood whenever I am shooting, not only to cut out flare and prevent stray light from entering the lens but also to protect it from knocks, which could damage the front element. Although most lenses come with a lens hood, they are not always adequate in certain lighting conditions. For this reason, I would recommend using a separate lens shield that is attached to the lens with a flexible arm. This can be varied to cope with extremely bright conditions and is more effective than a lens hood. Consider your own eyes when the sun is bright – it is a normal reaction to raise your hand to protect them or to wear a cap that has a large peak.

Lens extenders

A lens extender fits between the camera body and the lens. Depending on its strength, it increases the focal range of the lens. For example, if you're using a 200mm lens with a 2x extender, the effective focal length goes up to 400mm. Although this entails a loss of speed, giving an f/2.8 lens, say, a maximum aperture of only f/5.6, the portability of the extender and its low cost compared to that of a 400mm lens far outweigh this reduction.

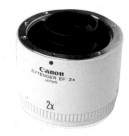

2x extender

Extension tubes and bellows

As well as an extender, I carry a set of extension tubes. Again, these fit between the camera body and the lens, and enable you to get extremely close to your subject. They normally come in sets of two and can be used individually or doubled up for greater magnification. However, once fitted, your lens will not be able to focus on infinity. Extension bellows perform a similar function but are bulkier and, therefore, more suited to indoor work.

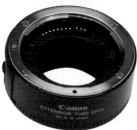

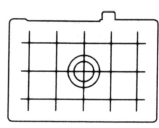

Extension tubes

Focusing screens

As you would expect from the vast DSLR camera system, there are more than just lens accessories to enhance your shooting capabilities. One such accessory is the focusing screen that is visible when you look through the eyepiece of the viewfinder. The benefits of interchangeable focusing screens are not just to aid focusing but also to help with composition. The grid screen does this particularly well, which is the reason why it is my favourite out of all the different screens. It has horizontal and vertical lines etched on to its surface and is

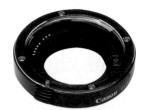

Grid screen

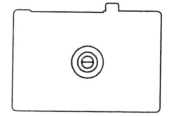

Cross-split image screen

An angle finder fitted over the viewfinder is useful when the angle of a shot is such that you can not look through the standard viewfinder.

invaluable for shooting most architectural subjects or where careful positioning of your subject in a particular area in the frame is essential.

With the cross-split image screen, the subject you are focusing on appears divided into two. As you focus the lens, the subject begins to merge and once it becomes pin sharp, only one image is visible. For precision focusing this screen is unbeatable; it is the kind of system that made the world-renowned Leica rangefinder camera so popular with professional photographers. Whatever screens you favour, you can easily interchange them yourself or ask a professional photographic dealer to do it for you.

Angle finders

DSLR cameras have interchangeable viewfinders. These are essential in certain situations when it's impossible to look through the camera using its standard viewfinder. For example, if your chosen viewpoint is at ground level or you are shooting in a confined space and the camera is back against a wall, you will not physically be able to look through the viewfinder. In such situations, an angle finder, fitted over the camera's viewfinder, lets you look down and view at right-angles to the camera eyepiece. These viewfinders are also very useful if your camera is mounted onto a copy stand for photographing images and/or flat artwork. The digital angle finder attaches to the eyepiece in a similar way but, instead of looking through an eyepiece, the image is displayed on an LCD, which is at right angles to the eyepiece. As well as being useful for shooting at ground level or in a confined space, this finder is invaluable when shooting in a

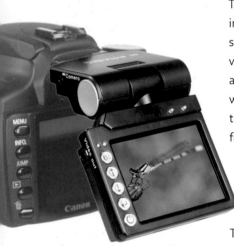

An alternative to the angle finder is the digital angle finder, which displays the image on an LCD. It is very useful for shooting in a confined space or at ground level.

crowd, where you might have to hold the camera at arm's length above your head. You can see what the lens is focusing on with the LCD display.

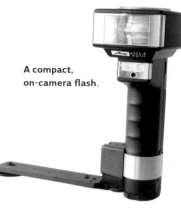

A compact, on-camera flash.

Flash

When most people think of camera accessories, flash is normally at the top of their list. While it is definitely a useful addition, flash needs to be used extensively and in many different situations before you can say that you have mastered it.

Many DSLR cameras have built-in flash, which is located at the top of the pentaprism and pops up when it is required. The benefits of such a unit are illustrated by its absence in the top-of-the-range cameras. Next time you see a group of photographers on the television news, observe how many use this type of flash. I guarantee that there won't be any because, quite frankly, the versatility and power of a built-in flash are completely inadequate. It would be far better to spend your money on a higher-spec camera and buy a separate flash-gun.

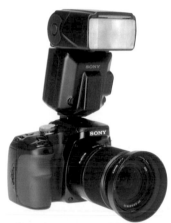

A much more powerful professional flash.

There are two main types of external flash. One fits on the top of the camera and is attached to the hotshoe. This requires no additional leads, unless you are using it off-camera, in which case a dedicated lead is slotted into the hotshoe at one end and the flash-gun at the other. The other type is usually mounted on a bracket and attached to the side of the camera. It is synchronized via a lead to a socket on the camera. This type of flash is usually much more powerful and, in some cases, several guns can be fired together.

Both these units can be used fully automatically when the camera is set to auto mode. This means

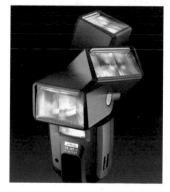

Detail of an on-camera flash in action, showing how the flash head swivels. Professional flash guns also have this facility.

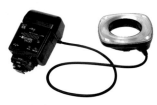

Ring flash

that the camera will read the flash output through the lens (TTL) and then adjust it or the aperture accordingly. You can also angle the head of the flash in a variety of different directions, so that you can 'bounce' the flash. Both units also have full manual override. DSLR cameras can synchronize flash only at shutter speeds of around 1/125 second – any faster than this speed will mean that some of the frame is unexposed.

The ring flash is another useful type of external flash. As the name suggests, it is made up of a circular flash tube that fits around the lens. Originally developed for medical and scientific photography, the ring flash gives a completely even light and creates a thin, faint shadow all around the subject. It is particularly useful for close-ups and, as with all your equipment, it needs a certain amount of experimentation in order to achieve the best results.

must know

Cable release
As you will normally be shooting at a slow shutter speed when using a tripod, it is a good idea to have a cable release to help you fire the shutter release more smoothly. If you fire it in the normal way with your finger, the camera can move, even if it's on a tripod.

Tripod

Although many people see tripods as burdensome, they are actually useful for many more reasons than just keeping the camera steady.

The first thing I look for in a tripod is rigidity. This might seem like stating the obvious but there are so many flimsy models available that would blow over in a gust of wind that they really are not worth bothering with. A good tripod should extend to a reasonable height and remain stable. Quick-release legs are preferable to screw versions, which can become cross-threaded and irreparable. Do make sure that the legs can be splayed at right angles to the head, which will enable you to shoot from low angles while keeping the camera steady.

Another useful addition is a central column. As well as giving additional height, this column can be inverted, which is an alternative method of getting a low-angle shot. On some models, this column can be attached at right angles to the tripod, which is a useful feature for close-up overhead photography. To top it off, purchase a good pan-tilt head so that the camera is free to move in a variety of directions.

Monopod

At an athletics meeting or a motor race, for example, where you are using an ultra-telephoto lens, such as a 400 or 600mm, a tripod might be inappropriate but you will still need some means of supporting the camera. These long lenses are almost impossible to hold steady, and their weight means that you need the arms of a bodybuilder. These are the occasions when I use a monopod. As its name suggests, the monopod has only one leg, and while it will not support the camera by itself, it will help to keep it steady.

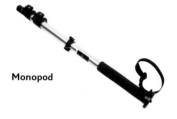

Monopod

Camera bag

Finally, you will need a good protective carrying case to keep your kit in. If I am travelling, I have all my equipment stored in a rigid flight case, which is foam-filled with cut-out compartments, so that each piece is held firm and is instantly visible. This is important because I can see immediately if anything is missing. When I am shooting outdoors, I transfer the appropriate equipment into a backpack. This leaves my hands free to hold the camera and take shots without having to put down and pick up the case repeatedly.

want to know more?

• Hire a DSLR before you buy one. It will save you money in the long run.
• Surf the Internet to get up-to-date information on the latest models and accessories. Go to: www.calumetphoto.co.uk
• Specialist magazines for photographers are always a good source of information. Look for: *Digital Photographer, The British Journal of Photography, Digital Camera*.

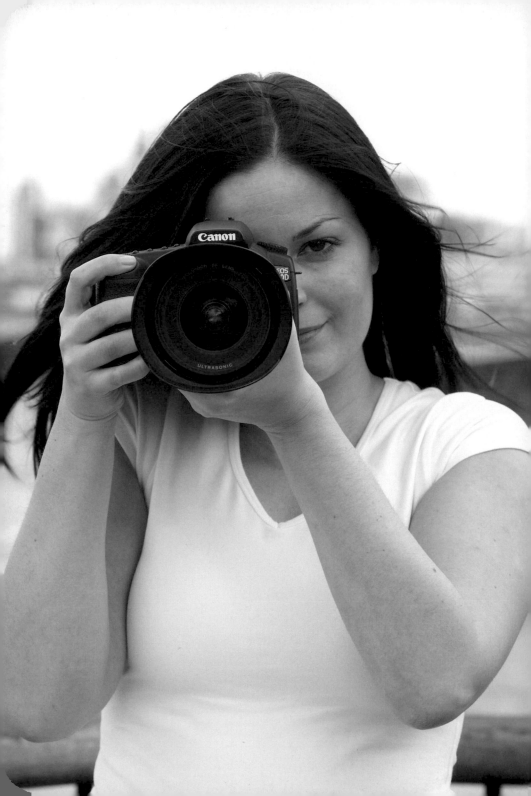

2 Getting to grips with your DSLR

Because DSLRs are more sophisticated than point and shoot cameras, it is worth discovering exactly what all of the controls and functions do before you start shooting. Taking time now will ensure that you will be getting the best out of all your equipment in any shooting situation. In this section, we guide you through the key areas, so that you are familiar with your kit.

DSLR basics

You're the proud owner of a new DSLR and, naturally, you can't wait to get out there and start snapping. Here are some simple tips and tricks to help you get the most from your new camera.

How to hold the camera

Holding the camera correctly so that you can use it freely at the same time as keeping it secure is most important. Hold the camera in your right hand, then allow the index finger of that hand to fall naturally over the shutter release. The control dial on the back should then line up easily with your thumb. Meanwhile, cradle the camera and lens barrel in the left hand with the palm uppermost, and wrap your fingers lightly around the zoom or focus ring of the lens. Now you're in complete control of your camera.

Holding a DSLR correctly makes it easier to use and helps keep it steady for each shot you take.

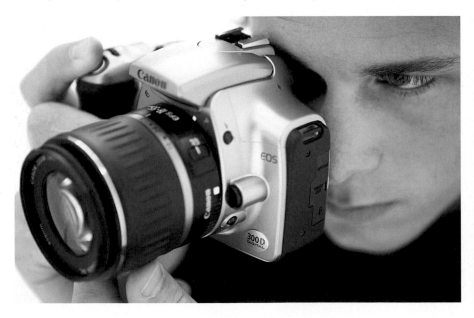

Fitting and charging batteries

It should come as no surprise to learn that a DSLR uses batteries to power its systems and allow you to take pictures. Most DSLRs use a single, rechargeable lithium-ion battery pack that is supplied with the camera, together with a charger.

It's important to give a new battery a full charge before you use it in the camera. The amount of time a full charge needs varies depending on the make and model of the camera/battery combination but, typically, expect at least a wait of a couple of hours. Check the camera's manual for specifics to be safe. To charge the battery, slot it into the charger (it will only go in one way) and plug the charger into a mains socket. A small LED will flash or glow, depending on the make of your camera/charger, indicating the charge is progressing.

Once charged, insert the battery into the camera. This may seem fiddly but it is really quite simple because, just as with the charger, the battery will go in only one way. A flap, which is usually on the camera's base, must be opened to reveal a cavity for the battery. Slot the battery home, close the lid and now you're ready to insert a memory card.

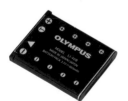

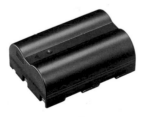

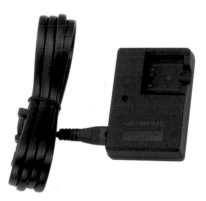

A DSLR memory card slots in only one way. Once in its special port, all your shots will be stored on this memory.

Whichever battery fits your camera, it can only slot home one way round: its shape means that you cannot get it wrong.

Many DSLRs are supplied with a special battery pack and charger, similar to the kit shown here. Always give a new battery a full charge before use.

Menus

DSLR menus might seem daunting at first but they are actually quite logical and, once you are familiar with them, you will be able to navigate to various settings quickly and easily.

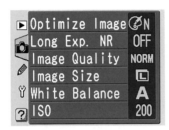

This menu from a Nikon D50 is typical of a display on a DSLR screen. The camera icon, which represents the shooting menu, is yellow to show it is active, and its settings are on display.

Navigating the menus

DSLRs use a system of menus displayed on their large screen to help you get at and set up many settings within the camera. Menus allow the external complexity of the camera to be simplified (there are fewer buttons) and specific items to be changed, such as setting the time or altering the compression when an image is saved to the memory card. More powerful options include changing how the focus system behaves in a given situation or selecting a specific image optimization setting, such as making colours in an image more vivid.

Most menus are set out in batches, just like a filing system, so all the shooting settings will be in one menu, while menus for playback preferences or general set-up settings, such as the date and time, will be in another 'file'. It pays to explore the menus on your camera with the manual to hand, so you can quickly familiarize yourself with the many options, what they do and when they might be needed. Most new DSLRs have a built-in help system that can be invoked to explain a particular menu or setting.

The importance of becoming familiar with these menus cannot be overstated since many of the more powerful tools in the camera's armoury are held within them. However, using the camera and not being afraid to experiment is the key to success.

Camera settings

All DSLRs have the equivalent of a point-and-shoot mode, where you turn on the camera, switch to auto-everything mode and away you go. But, eventually, you'll want to wrest control away from the camera and be more creative with it, or there may be a situation the auto-setting cannot cope with and you will need to take charge.

ISO (sensitivity)

The term ISO (International Standards Organization) was used originally as a rating to denote a camera film's sensitivity to light. For example, film with an ISO of 100 is less sensitive to light than that with an ISO of 400, and so on. Therefore, the higher the number, the gloomier the conditions you can shoot in without resorting to flash.

Noise is especially noticeable in this close-up from the image (below left). Extra processing on a computer would be needed to clean the image.

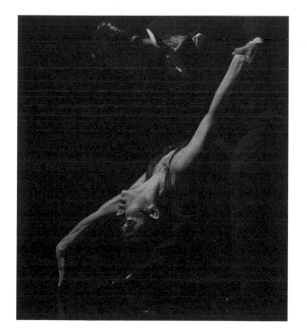

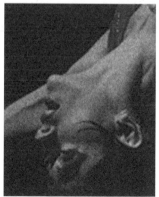

Getting a sharp shot of these flamenco dancers in low light required a sensitivity of ISO 1250 to ensure a fast-enough shutter speed. Such a high ISO has resulted in a picture replete with noise, visible as monochromatic dots and red and blue speckles.

must know

• **The higher the ISO, the greater the risk of 'noise'. If your camera has one, use the noise reduction setting from the menu.**
• **Light is 'warmer' at the beginning and end of the day.**
• **In indoor light, your shots will come out with an unwanted colour cast if you do not adjust your camera's WB from the daylight setting.**

Although there is no film in a DSLR, the term ISO is still used in digital photography to denote the sensitivity of the sensor. It's the same principle as with a film camera, except increasing the ISO of a DSLR increases the gain (think of it as the volume) of the sensor. Just as in film, the higher the ISO, the more sensitive the sensor becomes to light, but a downside (as with film) is that increasing the sensitivity can make images look 'grainier'. 'Grain' in digital terms is known as 'noise' since raising the ISO increases the chance of picking up 'noise' from non-image forming elements within the camera's system. Analogous to the static 'snow' on a TV that is not properly tuned, image noise typically makes its presence felt in areas of shots that are dark (the shadows), lighter areas (plain, grey skies) or in uniform areas of colour or areas that lack detail.

Establishing the ISO

The following ready reckoner shows when to use a particular ISO (sensitivity) setting and why, based upon typical DSLR sensitivity settings. Your camera may have more or fewer options available, but this guide works well as a rule of thumb:

• **ISO 100** Bright daylight, sunny conditions, hand-held shooting, with clean images (no noise) a priority.
• **ISO 200** As for ISO 100, but where a faster shutter speed or a slightly longer focal length is required and where you need extra flexibility with apertures and shutter speeds.
• **ISO 400** Indoor or slightly overcast conditions, where you want to avoid using flash or you need fast shutter speeds and full aperture control to shoot hand-held.

- **ISO 800** Overcast or dark indoor shooting, sports or action photography, where you need to freeze the motion, and noise issues are not paramount.
- **ISO 1250** Low light or indoors, long lens shooting (hand-held), but noise may become an issue.
- **ISO 1600** Night-time, low light, very long lens shooting; noise will almost certainly show in shots.
- **ISO 3200** As for ISO 1600, but where high shutter speeds are required; noise will be evident in shots.

White balance

The human eye and brain automatically compensate for the different colour temperatures of various light sources, so white always appears white to us. As DSLRs cannot do this, they have special settings to ensure white is white, no matter what the lighting conditions. If the WB (white balance) is not set correctly, it can make a difference to your shots and the off-colour casts created can ruin a photograph.

With a DSLR, you can quickly set the camera to, say, sunlight, cloudy conditions, tungsten lighting or fluorescent light, but there is also a separate easy-to-use manual setting, which you can save in the camera's memory to use again, thereby allowing you to tailor the WB even more closely to the lighting conditions.

Typically, you will need a piece of white paper illuminated by the lighting you want the camera to be set for. Filling the frame with a sheet of white paper and setting the WB to it (the exact process is usually straightforward but varies from camera to camera, so check your camera's manual) will mean that the camera can shoot ensuring that the whites are balanced and without any odd colour casts.

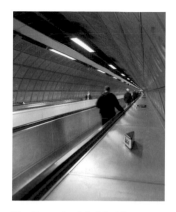

The fluorescent lighting has created an unnatural green colour cast across the entire image because an incorrect WB setting was used.

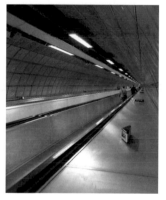

In this shot, taken at the same location seconds after the first image, the WB was set correctly and there's no colour cast.

must know

Know your WB settings:
- 1700–1800k
Match flame
- 2000–3000k
Sun: sunrise and sunset
- 2500–2900k
Household tungsten bulbs
- 3200–7500k
Fluorescent lights
- 5000–5400k
Sun: direct sun at noon
- 5500–6500k
Daylight: bright sun in a clear sky
- 6000–7500k
Overcast (cloudy) sky
- 7000–8000k
Outdoor shade

Although the human eye perceives daylight as 'white light', it is actually made up of lots of colours of light mixed together – in fact, all the colours of a rainbow. During the course of a day, the quality of light changes. At sunrise and sunset, for example, when the sun is visible, the light is said to be 'warm', or red, in colour. At noon, when the sun is at its highest, the light appears 'cool', or blue.

Kelvin scale

The variation in the colour of light is measured in Kelvins (so named after Lord William Kelvin who invented the scale in the mid-1800s by heating a block of carbon until it glowed, producing a range of colours as the temperature increased). The lower the Kelvin figure, the warmer, or redder, the colour; the higher the figure, the cooler, or bluer, the colour. DSLRs that allow you to adjust the WB take account of this colour shift and correct for it; some have a Kelvin scale adjustment for fine-tuning the settings.

File formats

DSLRs shoot images and save them on removable storage or memory cards. But the way the images are saved – the file format – has a significant bearing on image quality. DSLRs can typically shoot and save using the JPEG or TIFF compression file formats, although the latter is less popular, or the image data is left unprocessed as RAW files. JPEGs are processed inside the camera and then squashed down into a (much) smaller file size, thereby saving space on the memory card. The downside is JPEG compression loses detail; for that reason, it's known as a 'lossy' format. As the file is compressed, the

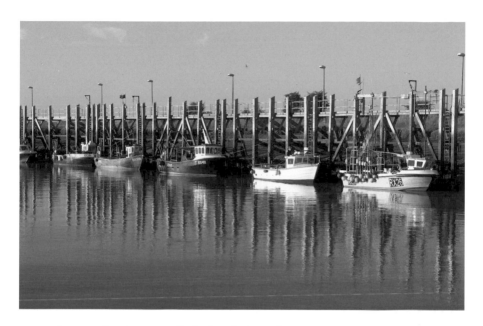

camera's computer removes self-similar pixels, such as large areas of blue in a landscape's sky, thereby reducing the size of the final, saved file. When the image is opened up on a computer, for example, it 'guesses' which pixels to replace, reducing image detail. JPEG files can be heavily compressed.

TIFF files are also compressed files, but they use a different compression method, allowing files to be reduced by up to around 50 per cent, but no more. This is a 'lossless' format, as no detail is lost. RAW is not a format as such but the raw, unprocessed image data from the camera. Its advantages include no compression and control of how the image looks – after the fact. With RAW files, the photographer carries out the processing – exposure, noise, white balance, even control of detail – later on a computer. Put simply, a RAW file is a digital negative and one of the photographer's most powerful tools.

The atmosphere in this shot is helped by the warm glow of the setting sun, which has quite a low Kelvin temperature of 2000k to 3000k. The same shot taken at noon in direct daylight, with a Kelvin temperature of around 5500k, would have a blue cast if the WB was not adjusted.

Interchangeable lenses

One of the key benefits of a DSLR is the versatility offered by interchangeable lenses, and no matter what make of DSLR you own, there is a set way to remove and replace your lenses.

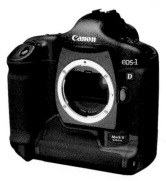

On this model of camera, the large lock/unlock lug, which must be pressed to release a mounted lens, is positioned to the right of the silver lens mount ring.

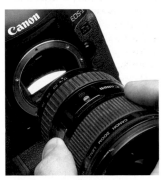

Indexes on the camera body and lens must be aligned when removing/attaching a lens from a DSLR. On this camera, the red dots need to be aligned.

Removing a lens

Typically, there is a button or lug alongside the lens that must be pressed to release the lens locking mechanism. Then you need to rotate the lens, either to the left or right (this depends on the make of camera) to release it from the lens mount and body. Make sure you replace the lens cap (and the body cap if you're not replacing the lens with another) to protect the delicate electrodes and mechanics of the lens's mounting system, prevent damage to the mount and stop dirt and dust reaching the sensor.

Attaching a lens

To attach a lens to the body, you must align indexes on the camera body and lens, bring the lens into contact with the mount and then rotate the lens (again, clockwise or anticlockwise, depending on your camera) to lock it home. It will click into place and won't budge once it's there. If it doesn't click or moves, then it's not locked home.

Do not force the lens onto the mount in the wrong position – you could damage the mount or lens – and don't touch any gold-coloured electrical contacts. Finger grease and sweat are slightly acidic and, as the contacts are the means of communication between the lens and camera, you really don't want them to corrode and stop working.

The viewfinder

Your view of the world through a DSLR is dominated by the viewfinder. Although what appears on the screen does vary a little from camera to camera, the image below shows the comprehensive information you can expect to see.

Viewfinder display

In the main viewing area of the diagram below, you can see the five AF (auto-focus) zones, which are shown as square brackets spread across the central portion of the screen. The memory card warning symbol illuminates if there is no card in the camera. The information in the black area covers a wide range of information, ranging from aperture and shutter speed in use to the number of images remaining on the memory card. The viewfinder display varies slightly from camera to camera.

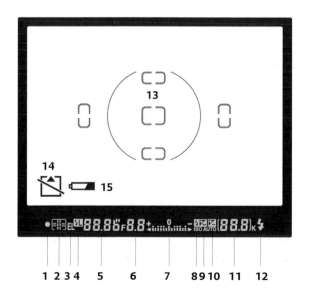

Across the viewfinder in the black zone, the following is displayed:

1 **Focus confirmation LED**
2 **AF area in use**
3 **Exposure lock**
4 **Flash needed warning/Flash status lock**
5 **Shutter speed**
6 **Aperture**
7 **Under-/overexposure and bracketing**
8 **Flash compensation**
9 **Auto-sensitivity indicator**
10 **Exposure compensation**
11 **Number of images/space (in kilobytes) left on memory card**
12 **Flash ready**
13 **AF zones**
14 **Memory card warning**
15 **Battery-life indicator**

Image and colour performance

Another key benefit of a DSLR – indeed, of almost all digital cameras, bar the most basic – is the control that you have over the way an image is treated by the camera's computer.

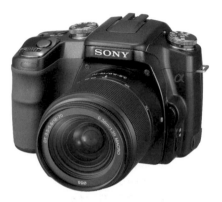

DSLRs, like this Sony Alpha 100, have powerful image performance enhancing settings, which allow you to predefine the colour parameters and image processing attributes, as well as the physical settings (shutter speeds and/or apertures, for example), all in advance of taking a shot.

Enhancing the image

All DSLRs allow you to alter and enhance the camera's image processing of a specific scene or colour set-up. For example, Canon's high-end professional DSLRs use a Colour Matrix set-up to help enhance colour by increasing or decreasing the saturation, and preset the colour performance for a type of subject, typically portraits, or for a specific colour space.

Preset modes

DSLRs aimed more at consumers than pros have presets for colour performance, such as Standard, Vivid, Sunset and Portrait, and for specific scenes. These modes can set the camera for specific subjects rather than a type of colour performance. Scene modes, such as Portrait, Landscape, Macro and Sports, allow you to set the camera quickly to get the most from the subject, automatically setting it to its optimal settings (including shutter, aperture and metering) for the selected scene. You can use them in conjunction with the colour settings, if required. The camera applies special processes to captured images and optimizes the attributes you've selected to enhance them. Unless you know from experience what these settings offer, you will need to experiment: a vivid setting on one shot of flowers may look artificial on a portrait picture.

Exposure

The metering modes, exposure compensation and bracketing are some of the more powerful controls at your fingertips on a DSLR. Using them to fine-tune your images helps you to create shots that look exactly as you want them.

Metering modes

A DSLR can measure the light for a given scene in a variety of ways. It has a matrix of light sensors, or meters, that covers the area you see through the viewfinder to give a general light reading. Even though it has a large number of zones to measure light from, it can also do it using smaller, specific areas of the frame.

There are three main modes of metering: matrix (multi-zone or honeycomb), centre-weighted and spot metering. Matrix uses all the metering zones the camera has at its disposal (the number varies according to the model and manufacturer) and measures an average of all the zones to give the 'as metered' exposure value. Centre-weighted metering is, as the name suggests, where the light in only the central portion of the frame is measured. The third mode, spot metering, is where a small, central spot of the subject or scene is metered; in some cameras, you can adjust the size of the 'spot' yourself from, say, a four per cent (in area) 'spot' to an eight per cent 'spot' in the centre of the frame.

The advantages of one method of metering over another depend on the subject being photographed but, broadly speaking, matrix metering works well for most shooting situations. Centre-weighted

must know

- When shooting portraits with strong backlighting, use the centre-weighted, or spot, mode.
- Auto-bracketing is useful when working under pressure.
- With spot metering you can check the light in specific areas of your shot to ascertain the best exposure.
- DSLRs have a wide exposure latitude, but there is nothing like getting the right exposure to begin with.

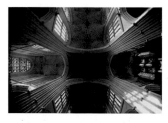

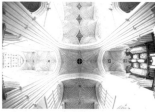

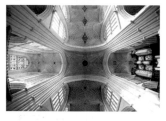

This sequence shows how you can automatically bracket around the metered exposure for a shot to provide more choice later on. The exposures shown (from top to bottom) are as follows: one stop underexposure, one stop overexposure, and as metered.

metering is ideal for complex lighting, or where there are areas of deep shade or light and you want to bias exposure to one or the other. Spot metering allows you to meter precisely from a small area, making it ideal for portraits or macro work, where it's important to get the metering spot on.

Exposure compensation

Exposure compensation is a method of fine-tuning the exposure of a scene by compensating for overly bright or dark areas. This is done by, typically, up to three stops of exposure, depending on the type of DSLR you have. Set using a specific control on the camera, exposure compensation can be applied to one image at a time, or until you reset the compensation feature back to its 'as-metered' exposure level, where there is no compensation.

Auto-bracketing

Automatic exposure bracketing can be thought of as an insurance policy for your snaps. It is similar to exposure compensation in that it changes the exposure to a predefined level and for the same reasons, but when an image is shot, the camera will automatically shoot one image (or more, depending on the camera) at the set amount of overexposure and one at the same set amount of underexposure. You'll get three (or more, depending on the camera) images, one of the correct 'as-metered' exposure, one underexposed by, say, half a stop and one overexposed by the same amount, depending on how you've set the camera. Then you can decide later (on the camera screen or on the computer, for example) which is the best for the subject.

Using auto-focus (AF)

One of the key factors affecting the success of any shot is how sharply focused it is, even though you may sometimes want creative blur or an unfocused look. Whatever the shot, DSLRs have special focusing modes to help produce the desired effect.

Single and continuous modes

In essence, the Single AF mode sets the AF system to find the main subject in a scene, focus upon it and then lock. This makes it ideal for static subjects. Continuous AF, on the other hand, finds the subject and (depending on what camera you have) tracks its movement. A special predictive AF set-up ensures that when the shutter eventually fires, the subject captured is sharp.

Other AF tools

Both focus modes (above) can work in conjunction with another powerful AF tool found on DSLRs, the AF Area Mode. Here, the type, number and shape of the AF zones that will be active are controlled. Typically, there is a Single Area AF, where just one AF zone works at a time, and a Dynamic AF (sometimes referred to as Servo AF), which allows just one, a whole group or all the AF zones to work together simultaneously – this helps when you are shooting complex or moving subjects and adds to focus accuracy. Some DSLRs have a Closest Subject Priority AF, which will always try to focus on the main part of the scene closest to the camera. This is particularly useful when there is a cluttered or possibly distracting background.

must know

If you want to take control of the focusing chores on a DSLR, you can. Most AF lenses allow you to override the AF manually at any time, or you can turn off the AF, if required. To do this, there will be an on/off switch on the camera body and/ or on the lens.

Shutter or aperture priority

With a DSLR you can choose to have either aperture priority or shutter priority. Which you choose will depend on the type of shot you are going to take and the effect that you wish to create.

How and when to use

The mode dial of a DSLR has a range of automatic settings and a manual setting ('M'). There are two other controls: aperture priority ('A', or 'Av') and shutter priority ('S', or 'Tv', which denotes time value). When one of these controls is selected, the camera will automatically adjust the other in order to keep a properly metered exposure. Simply put, if you need to control the depth of field but shutter speeds are less of an issue – as, for example, when the camera is tripod-mounted

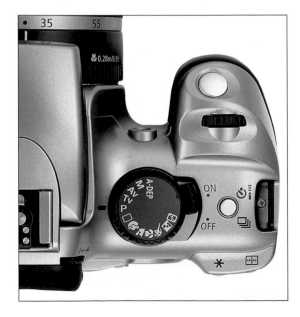

This image shows the mode dial on a DSLR with the automatic settings on view, plus 'Av' and 'Tv' (aperture and shutter priority) settings. The 'M' setting is the manual control for the apertures and shutters, as required.

for a macro shot – you should use aperture priority. You can then select the best aperture for the required depth of field while the camera takes care of the shutter speed.

Shutter priority

If shutter speed control is paramount for you – for example, if you need to ensure a fast shutter speed in order to freeze an action shot – then select shutter priority. While you ensure the shutter speed is fast enough, the camera sets an aperture to keep the shot correctly metered for the scene.

Depth of field preview

When you look through the viewfinder of your DSLR the lens views the scene at 'wide open'. This means that the lens is at its maximum aperture even if you have stopped the lens down to a smaller aperture. DSLR cameras have a small button on the camera body, which is usually adjacent to the lens, that, when pressed, shuts the aperture to the current setting – this is the depth of field (DOF) preview control. With the DOF preview button depressed, the aperture of the lens closes to its current setting (if it is smaller than the maximum aperture), thus allowing you to look through the viewfinder and to assess how much of the scene will be sharp from in front of the lens to the distance.

A large aperture, that is a low f/number, such as f/2.8, gives a very narrow DOF, which means that the subject will be sharp, but everything behind and in front of it will be blurred. A higher f/number, say, f/22, will give a deep DOF, resulting in a sharp foreground and background.

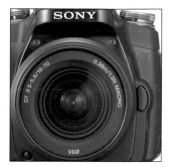

The button at the bottom left corner of this DSLR is the DOF preview button. Pressing it will stop the lens to the metered or selected aperture, enabling accurate assessment of the DOF.

want to know more?

• Go to Google to look for websites relating to specific areas of interest.
• Join a camera club and meet fellow enthusiasts to share your interests and knowledge.
• Make sure you read the manufacturer's manual for your DSLR to familiarize yourself with all its functions.
• Keep up with the latest kit. Look in the specialist magazines.

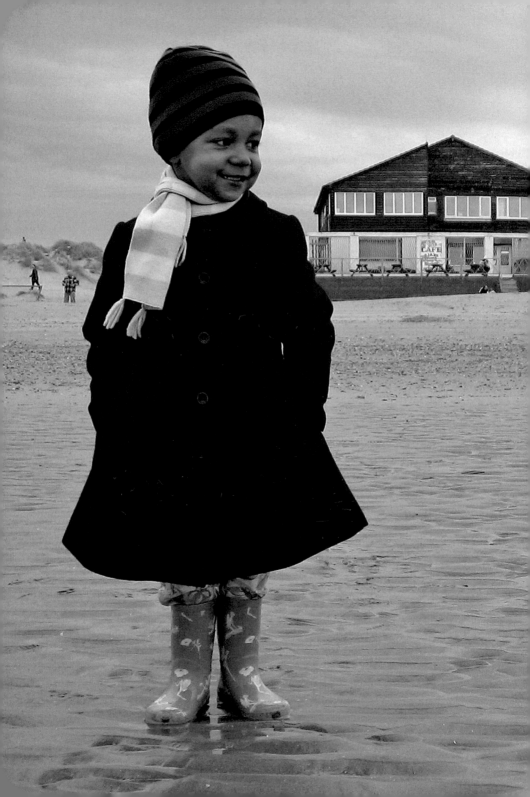

3 Seeing the picture

Many people find they are disappointed with their photographs because they never seem to come out in the way in which the shot is remembered. The reason for this is that the camera does not see things in the same way as the eye. However, cameras and their lenses have a distinct advantage over the eye in the sense that you can either zoom in or out, or change the lens. This means that you can bring distant objects nearer, to see greater detail, or include a wider angle of view.

The golden section

If you want your pictures to stand out, there are a few simple rules that will give you the basis for perfectly composed pictures every time you shoot. These rules, which have been followed by artists down the generations, are all based on the principle usually known as the golden section, or the rule of thirds.

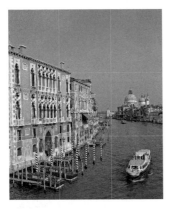

When composing shots, try to imagine a grid like the one here. If you place your subject at the intersection of imaginary lines drawn vertically and horizontally one-third of the way in from the sides of the picture, you will have a well-balanced composition.
> Canon EOS 1DS, 50mm lens, 1/125 sec, f/8.

What is the golden section?

It was the Ancient Greek mathematician Euclid who first espoused the principle of the golden section. The theory of this ratio dictates that the subject of a picture or photograph be placed at the intersection of imaginary lines drawn vertically and horizontally one-third of the way along the sides of a picture. Sculptors and architects have followed the principle to produce classically proportioned statues and buildings. The mathematician Pythagoras proved that the golden section was the basis for the proportions of the human figure, showing that the body is built with each part in a golden proportion to all other parts. During the Italian Renaissance, Leonardo da Vinci adopted and perfected this theory.

Following the principle

There are important elements to consider every time you compose your pictures, and all of them relate to the principle of the golden section. The first of these is framing the picture. Ask yourself if the shot would look better taken with the camera held in landscape mode or turned vertically in its portrait mode. The second is viewpoint – explore whether you should change it from a high viewpoint

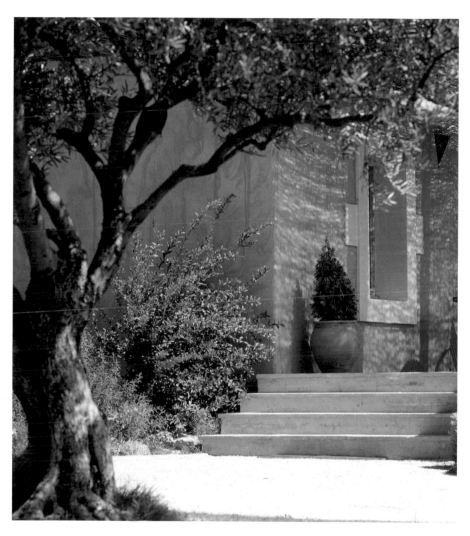

to a low one or vice versa. You need to pay attention also to the foreground and background and how to make them work within the overall composition. Since a DSLR camera with its lenses can zoom in and out, crop and include, blur and keep sharp, you can use it to control and enhance all the elements that go into making up the overall composition.

Here the tree frames the shot, occupying the left-hand and top-third of the picture. This gives a strong balance and leads the eye into the centre of the shot.
> Canon EOS 1DS, 28mm lens, 1/125 sec, f/16.

Framing the picture

Probably the greatest advantage of a DSLR camera is that when you look through the viewfinder, what you see is exactly what the lens sees. This is the most accurate way of viewing your subject, which should make it easy to frame your shot perfectly.

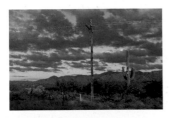

The telegraph pole and cactus look lost in landscape mode.

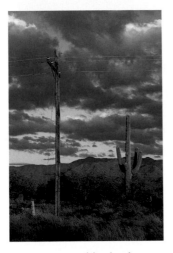

A tighter composition has been achieved in portrait mode.
> Canon EOS 1DS, 70mm lens, 1/50 sec, f/11.

Taking your time

Even with this advantage, many people develop the unfortunate habit of always having their subject in the middle of the frame and shooting with the camera in its landscape (horizontal) mode. Usually this because they don't give enough time and thought to placing the subject in its optimum position.

Placing your subject slap in the middle of the frame often fails to produce the best picture because there can be too much distracting detail surrounding it. Using the landscape mode to shoot a portrait also results in unwanted peripheral detail. The human face fits far more comfortably in portrait mode, and you can zoom in and literally fill the frame – all you need do is turn the camera 90°. Many DSLR cameras have duplicated controls, so the shutter release button is as easy to reach in landscape or portrait mode.

Photographs for publication

Many professionals compose their pictures with an idea already in mind of how they might be published. For example, they may compose their shots to fit over two pages in a magazine or book. When doing this, it is important that the gutter (where two facing pages join in the middle), which may have to slice through the shot, is in a position that is not

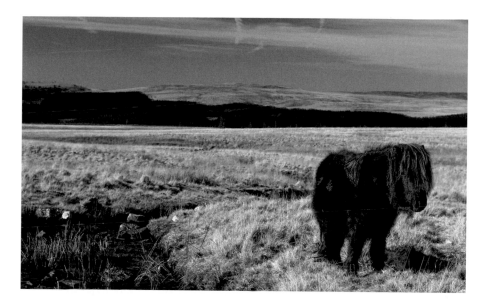

going to affect the main subject. If you are hoping to have your pictures published, consider where the gutter or type might be positioned. Consider, too, where the type might go on a double-page spread image. If the shots had been taken without enough of a neutral area, the type would be illegible.

I deliberately placed this pony to one side of the frame, as I thought it might make a double-page picture in a magazine. The gutter would fall in a neutral area of the shot and there is enough blue sky for some type to be dropped in.
> Canon EOS 1DS, 28mm lens, 1/60 sec, f/11.

Professional tips

Below are some useful tips to help you when you are framing your photographs.

- Do not be afraid to go in close to your chosen subject and fill the whole frame.
- Change the lens if you can't get in close enough. Cropping the picture on the computer at a later date will only result in a loss of quality.
- Always look at your subject with the camera in both portrait and landscape modes.
- Try a few shots where your subject is to one side of the frame and not just in the middle.

Viewpoint

Selecting the best viewpoint for a shot is often low down in the list of priorities because, having seen a view of a subject that we find attractive, many of us shoot from that very spot. In some cases this might work, but if we had given ourselves just a little more time, the shot might have been so much better.

must know

- Explore all the angles. Moving just a few paces away from your chosen viewpoint can make a difference to the shot.
- If using a zoom lens, altering the focal length could improve your shot enormously, even from the same viewpoint.
- You may have the best viewpoint but the shot could be enhanced at a different time of day.
- Crouch down and use a low viewpoint. It could improve the perspective.

Important questions

Having chosen what you are going to shoot, take your time to look at the subject and then ask yourself the following questions:
- From where I'm standing, is the sun in the best possible position?
- Are there any unattractive shadows dominating the picture?
- Is there any foreground interest?
- Are there any features in the foreground that can be used to enhance the overall composition?
- Is the background interesting? Does it overpower the main subject?
- Am I seeing the most attractive features?
- Have I chosen the right focal length of lens or adjusted my zoom?
- Would the shot look better if I took it from a lower or a higher viewpoint?
- Is there is a better angle for taking the shot?
  This may seem an intimidating list of questions but the fact that you have chosen to use a DSLR camera indicates that you want your shots to look special. After all, if you bought a Ferrari, would you use it only for the weekly shop? No, you would want to explore its full potential.

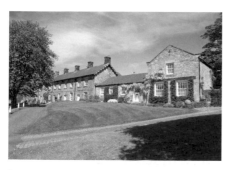

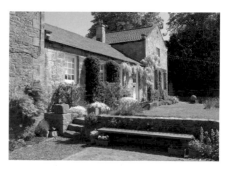

I was attracted to this terrace of houses, particularly the one with wisteria growing over its walls. I took my shot but realized that I'd done so from the worst possible viewpoint: there is too much uninteresting foreground, half of which is in deep shadow, the wisteria is hardly visible and the 24mm lens has made the shot too wide-angled.

I then moved around the building and chose another viewpoint. Although this focused more on the house with the wisteria, the background was still in deep shadow, as were the steps. In addition, the wall on the left was uninteresting and, even though I had reduced the focal length to 35mm, there was still too much unwanted material in the shot.

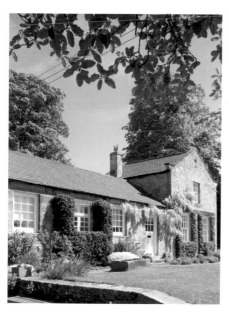

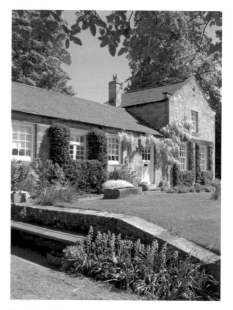

Here, I moved to the right, facing the house more 'full on'. This cropped out the oppressive background, as well as the wall on the left, but the small wall in the foreground didn't add anything and the power lines irritated me.

For the final shot, I moved more to the right. A higher viewpoint meant I could disguise the power lines with branches, and I could include the bluebells in the foreground.

> Canon EOS 1DS, 24mm lens, 1/100 sec, f/11.

Foregrounds

Invariably, it is the foreground of a shot that will first attract the viewer's attention, and it's therefore important that you give whatever occupies this part of the frame due consideration.

Creating interest

Placing an item of interest in the foreground of your overall composition will help to give it balance, as well as being a tool to lead the eye into the picture. However, it's important not to place an item in the same part of the frame, such as the bottom right-hand corner, in all your shots, otherwise they will take on a familiarity that will become monotonous to the viewer, especially if your shots are presented together in a folio or album.

Although tradition would have us placing the foreground interest to one side of the frame, there is no reason why a shot should not work with the point of interest placed centrally. This is true when an element of symmetry is required or when the foreground is to occupy at least half of the entire frame. Choosing a dominant foreground can help to reduce clutter in the composition because all its detail will be clear, while the background will just be hinted at, even though it might be quite sharp.

Wide-angle v. telephoto

Depth of field is greater with a wide-angle lens, so you will be able to keep items that are quite close to the lens as sharp as those placed further away. This will give them greater prominence in the foreground. Be careful that working at such close

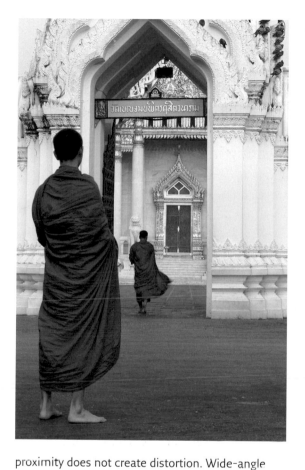

I used a telephoto lens and a small aperture to get maximum depth of field for this picture. The monk in the foreground is the focus of interest; the one in the middle distance helps lead the eye into the rest of the shot.
> Canon EOS 1DS, 100mm lens, 1/15 sec, f/22.

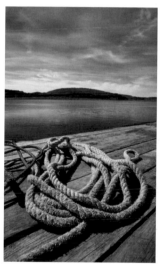

I chose a low viewpoint for this shot, to emphasize the ropes and jetty in the foreground. The texture of the rope adds interest , while the boards of the jetty give a strong sense of perspective.
> Canon EOS 1DS MK2, 24mm lens, 1/125 sec, f/8.

proximity does not create distortion. Wide-angle lenses can create the illusion of greater space between the foreground and the background, so always make sure that distant objects do not become so small that they are difficult for the eye to read. For this reason it might be preferable to use a telephoto lens. You will then be able to keep the foreground interest prominent, while appearing to reduce the distance of the background. As with any combination of lens and foreground, viewpoint will be of paramount importance.

Backgrounds

If foregrounds can help lead the eye into a shot, then backgrounds can create the backdrop to set off the subject. Whatever you are shooting, it is always possible to alter how the background will appear, whether you are taking portraits or landscapes.

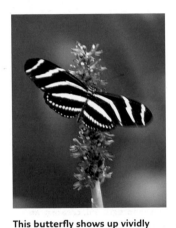

This butterfly shows up vividly against a blurred background. I used a 200mm telephoto and 2x extender to give an effective focal length of 400mm. The purple flower and green stem give an interesting splash of colour.
> Canon EOS 1DS MK2, 200mm lens, 2x extender, 1/30 sec, f/5.6.

Altering the background

The background of a shot can often appear so far away in the distance that it seems impossible to alter it. However, by choosing the correct viewpoint and the appropriate focal length lens and aperture, it can be enhanced in many different ways.

Softening and sharpening

When photographing outdoors, you will probably want to soften the background, to place the emphasis firmly on your subject. A medium telephoto lens in the region of 100–200mm, set to its widest possible aperture to reduce the depth of field, is ideal for this. With a wide-angle lens, you will have less control over the background because it keeps more of the picture in focus, even at wide apertures.

Sometimes it is desirable to keep the background as sharp as possible, either because it is telling you about the subject or making a point about the environment. A wide-angle lens is probably the best choice for this as it keeps more of the shot in focus. If you use a telephoto lens, you may need to stop the aperture right down to give as much depth of field as possible. A telephoto lens foreshortens the picture and makes the distances between near and far objects appear less than they are.

Previewing the shot

Shooting with a DSLR means that you have the advantage of using the depth of field preview, which allows you to see what a shot will look like after stopping down the lens. This is important, as something in the background that might not be apparent at full aperture – how we see through the viewfinder – could appear to be growing out of your subject's head when the lens is stopped down.

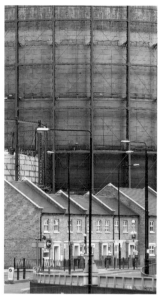

I waited quite some time for this gasometer to fill and take up the entire background. I liked the way it towered over the houses in the foreground, creating an oppressive, claustrophobic feel.
> Canon EOS 1DS MK2, 200mm lens, 1/100 sec, f/8.

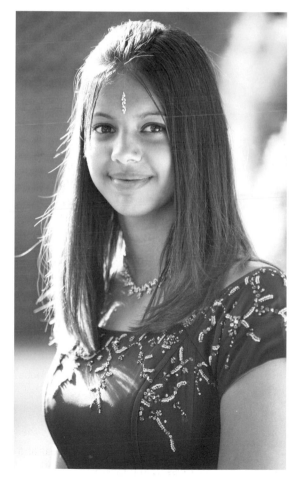

Softening the background for an outdoor portrait, so it does not detract from the subject, is often desirable. This background is a mottled blend of greens that contrasts with the pink dress. If using auto-focus, ensure that the sensor is on the eyes.
> Canon EOS 1DS MK2, 70-200mm zoom lens, 1/125 sec, f/8.

Depth of field

DSLR cameras will give you far greater control over depth of field than compact cameras, which means that you can be much more creative with your photographic compositions.

What is depth of field?

Depth of field (DOF) relates to the overall sharpness of your picture. Whatever the aperture, there is an area immediately in front of and behind the point that you have focused on that is sharp. It is this area that we refer to as the depth of field.

With a wide aperture, such as f/2.8, very little behind the point of focus, and even less in front of that point, is sharp. While this shallow area of sharp focus can be put to good effect for certain shooting situations, in others it can be a disadvantage. If you stop the lens down, for example to an aperture of f/8, more of the area in front of the point of focus, and even more behind it, will be sharp. If you stop down even further, for example to an aperture of f/22, an even greater area of the shot will be sharp. Stopping the lens down necessitates a slower shutter speed, but this might mean that if you have an aperture of f/22, the shutter speed required will be too slow for you to hold the camera steady, even if you are using a lens with IS (image stabilizing).

Focal lengths

Depth of field varies with lenses of different focal lengths. For example, if using a 24mm wide-angle lens, the area of sharp focus will be quite large, even without stopping the lens right down. With a

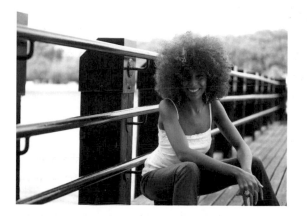

I took this sequence from the same viewpoint with the same camera and lens but varied the aperture to show how it affects the depth of field and the impact of the composition. At f/2.8, the rails in the foreground are out of focus, as are the rails and trees in the background, so the eye focuses on the model.
> Canon EOS 1DS MK2, 70mm lens, 1/400 sec, f/2.8.

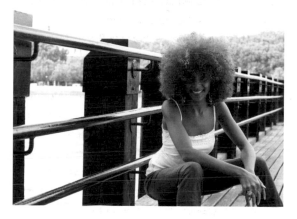

By stopping the lens down to f/8, both the foreground and background are sharper.
> Canon EOS 1DS MK2, 70mm lens, 1/50 sec, f/8.

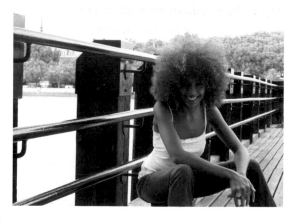

At f/22, virtually the entire shot is sharp, making it more difficult to focus attention on the model.
> Canon EOS 1DS MK2, 70mm lens, 1/6 sec, f/22.

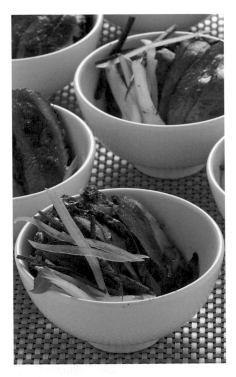
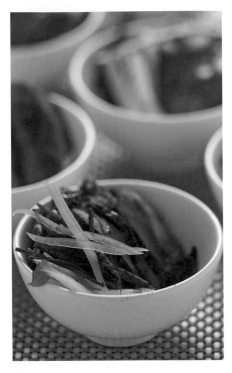

I wanted to show as many dishes as possible in this still life (above left) and for them to be sharp, so I stopped the lens down to f/22. I was quite close to the subject, so the depth of field wasn't as great as it might have been.
> **Canon EOS 1DS MK2, 150mm lens, 1/50 sec, f/8.**

When I opened up the lens to f/2.8 (above right), the emphasis shifted to the foreground dish, leaving the others blurred. Both shots are valid, but this one focuses the eye on the food.
> **Canon EOS 1DS MK2, 150mm lens, 1/60 sec, f/2.8.**

50mm lens, the area of sharp focus will decrease, even at the same aperture. With a telephoto lens, the area of sharp focus is even more reduced. If you are using the camera's 'aperture priority' setting, you can select the aperture manually while the camera automatically selects the shutter speed.

Far from being a drawback, these variations in depth of field can be put to good effect: you can isolate your subject and make it stand out from the background, particularly when taking portraits, where a sharp background can be a distraction.

DSLRs always show the image in the viewfinder at wide open, so use the depth of field preview to determine what area will be in sharp focus and what its effect will be on the overall composition.

The shutter

The shutter governs the amount of time the light is allowed to pass through the lens onto the sensor. Having two different methods of controlling the light exists for specific reasons and not just for exposure control, although there is a correlation between the speed of the shutter and the size of the aperture.

Blurring and freezing movement

I have explained how the aperture can control the depth of field and therefore the overall sharpness of the picture. Here, you will see how the shutter can control the degree of sharpness by either blurring or freezing the movement in your pictures.

The shutter range on most DSLR cameras is quite extensive, with 30 seconds to 1/8000 of a second not uncommon. There are usually one-third increments in between the main shutter speeds: for instance, there are two other available speed settings between 1/30 and 1/60. With such a huge choice, you should be able to cope with any shooting situation.

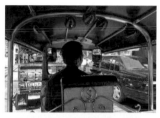

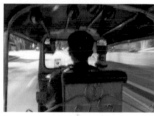

Photographed with a shutter speed of 1/60 sec, this Bangkok tuk-tuk appears motionless (top). Changing the shutter speed to 1/8 sec (above) conveys the speed and bumpiness of the ride.
> Canon EOS 1DS, 24mm lens, 1/8 sec, f/22.

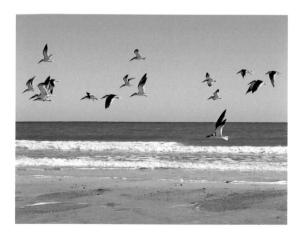

To keep the movement of the birds and water sharp, I chose a shutter speed of 1/1000 sec. A slow shutter speed would have blurred any movement and made the birds unrecognizable.
> Canon EOS 1DS, 70mm lens, 1/1000 sec, f/11.

I took this shot in available light, setting the ISO to 800, so the shutter speed would be fast enough to keep the barman and drinks sharp. This has increased the noise level, but is still within the bounds of what is acceptable.
> Canon EOS 1DS, 100mm lens, 1/125 sec, f/2.8.

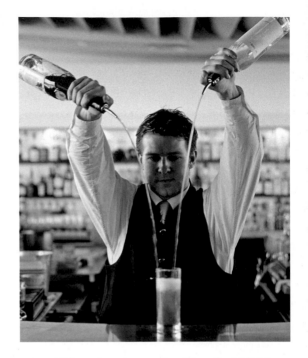

must know

• Try using different shutter speeds to vary your shots. A slow speed may seem inappropriate but it may result in the most evocative image.
• Long exposures may increase the level of noise; select the noise reduction function before you shoot.
• Camera batteries drain rapidly at the 'B' setting, so have some spare batteries to hand.
• To avoid camera shake at slow shutter speeds (even on a tripod) use the mirror up facility and a cable release.

In addition, there is a setting 'B', or 'bulb'. With this, the shutter remains open for as long as the shutter release is held down. This is used most commonly for night shots and situations where the light levels are extremely low and a long exposure is required. However, such exposures may result in an unacceptably high degree of noise, so if your camera is fitted with a noise reduction function, set it.

When shooting a moving object, such as a bird in flight, use a fast shutter speed to 'freeze' the motion. This would be at least 1/250 sec, although 1/500 or 1/1000 is not unusual. Anything slower will result in the bird becoming blurred. Another reason for using a fast shutter speed is to eliminate camera shake. This can happen even when your subject is static because it is you who is moving.

Perspective

One of the essential elements of a good photograph is a sense of perspective. Since photographs are two-dimensional, it is down to you, the photographer, to create a feeling of space and depth between the various objects that make up your shot.

Lenses and perspective

The lens you choose can help create this sense of perspective: wide-angle lenses give an appearance of greater space between near and far objects, while telephoto lenses seem to reduce the distance. Of course, this is an illusion: if you took a shot of the same subject with two lenses of different focal lengths and enlarged the wide-angle one so that it was cropped the same as the telephoto version, the

Below left: A 70mm lens gives the appearance of perspective as the jetty tapers away.
> Canon EOS 1DS, 70mm lens, 1/250 sec, f/11.

Below: Taking the shot from the same viewpoint with a 28mm lens makes the jetty seem longer than it is, which gives the picture a greater sense of perspective.
> Canon EOS 1DS, 28mm lens, 1/250 sec, f/11.

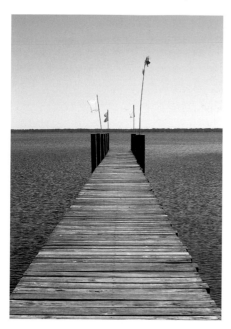 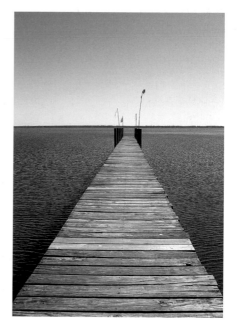

must know

• When pointing the camera upwards your subject will appear taller than it really is.
• Wide-angle lenses give the illusion of greater perspective.
• Use a framing device, such as an arch, wall or tree, in the foreground to increase the sense of depth in your shot.

compression would appear the same. Obviously, the quality of the wide-angle shot would suffer because the degree of enlargement required would increase the noise and reduce the sharpness of the image.

Changing viewpoint

It's also possible to create a sense of depth by choosing a viewpoint that increases the distance from the foreground of your shot to the background. You can use something in the foreground to lead the eye into the picture, as demonstrated in the shot below of buildings in the Barbican, London. Using foregrounds in this way greatly increases the feeling of depth, or perspective.

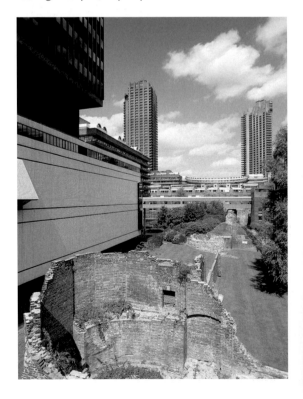

I chose this viewpoint so the wall of the modern building would act as the tool to lead the eye into the shot. The ancient wall in the foreground is an important element of the composition as your eyes shift their focus from it to the more modern architecture.
> Canon EOS 1DS, 28mm lens, 1/125 sec, f/11.

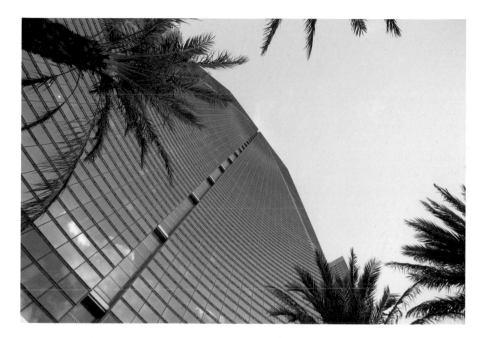

Photographed from a close viewpoint with the camera pointed up, this building appears a lot taller than it really is. This is because it tapers towards the top, increasing the illusion of perspective. Shots that are taken in this way can can look more dynamic than those where all the verticals appear strictly vertical.
> Canon EOS 1DS, 17mm lens, 1/85 sec, f/5.

The angle at which you hold the camera is another way of enhancing the sense of perspective. If you look at a building from a distance so that the viewpoint is straight on, it could be argued that it looks its 'normal' height. However, if you move in closer and change your viewpoint so that you are looking upwards, the building will appear to taper towards the top. This phenomenon is known as converging verticals and it will make the building look taller than it actually is. A wide-angle lens will increase this effect even more.

want to know more?

• Go to photographic exhibitions in galleries to see how the top professionals do it. Details are available on the Internet and in national newspapers.
• On days out, at places of interest, always try to find a different angle for your shot.
• All magazines are a source of inspiration, so have a browse.

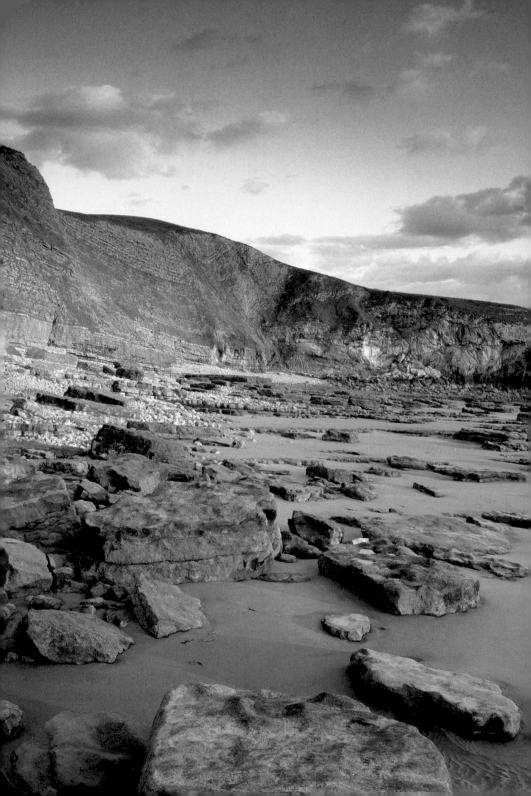

4 Landscapes

The variety of challenges posed by shooting landscapes, especially changing light and unpredictable weather, means it's important that you are as well equipped as possible. But since you might have to carry your kit for long distances, keep the weight to a minimum. Shooting landscapes can be one of the most rewarding areas for a photographer. However it's not just the view; there are considerations such as the season, climate and time of day. Whether it's on your own doorstep or far away, a good landscape photograph will be remembered forever.

Summer

Most of us look forward to summer with longer daylight hours, sunshine and warmth, but hazy skies and glaring light mean conditions are not always ideal for photographing landscapes.

Light and shadows

My preferred times of day for shooting in bright summer light are first thing in the morning and late afternoon or early evening, when the sun creates long shadows that add interest and texture to landscapes. To capture such scenes in the morning often entails getting up early, even before the sun has risen. Once it comes over the horizon, it rises extremely rapidly, and you won't have long to take your shots – if you're not quick, you will miss out on the best light and lose the optimum shot. Towards the end of the day, you are fighting against fading light, so being in position beforehand is vital. Take your shots early on in summer – you never know when a field of golden wheat will be harvested!

As the sun climbs in the sky, shadows become shorter, with less contrast to a scene, and this high, bright light rarely suits landscape photography. This is especially true in expansive landscapes, such as farmland fields, deserts or seascapes, where foreground interest is in short supply.

The light first thing in the morning and towards the end of the day tends to be warm, which creates tremendous atmosphere in your shots. It's essential to set the camera's WB (white balance) manually; automatic white balance (AWB) may neutralize the scene and the warm atmosphere will be lost.

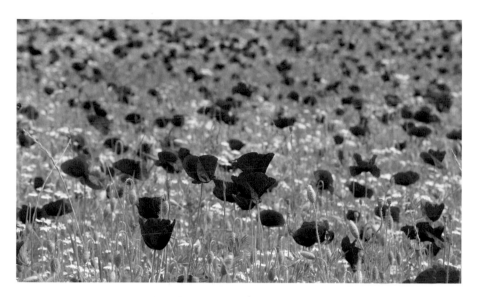

For this shot I made sure that the flowers in the foreground took prominence by using a wide aperture, which reduced the area of sharp focus.
> Canon EOS 1DS, 200mm lens, 1/500 sec, f/2.8.

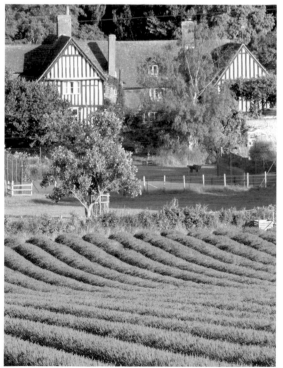

Strong shadows last for only a short time first thing in the morning, so get up early to take advantage of them. As well as casting noticeable shadows on the roof here, the sun has clearly defined the rows of lavender.
> Canon EOS 1DS MK2, 400mm lens, 1/6 sec, f/22.

Autumn

This season is probably the shortest for photographers, so make sure you plan ahead. Autumn is unpredictable: its beauty depends on the summer just past, when a lack of rain can cause leaves to brown early without ever turning a golden hue. They can also fall from the trees before the season has really started.

Changing colours

The colour of trees in autumn can be breathtaking, with strong sunlight making all the difference to the impact of your shots. A deep blue sky acting as a backdrop to a tree covered in rich golden-red leaves is particularly striking. A polarizing filter will help to deepen the blue of the sky, and it's best to take your pictures early in the morning when the shadows are deep and long, adding drama to your compositions. Later in the day, when the sun is higher, this effect will be lost because the shadows are much shorter.

The strength of this simple composition lies in the contrast between the rich colours of the foliage and the deep blue sky. I took the shot early in the morning and used a polarizing filter to deepen the colour of sky.
> **Canon EOS 1DS, 17mm lens, 1/100 sec, f/11.**

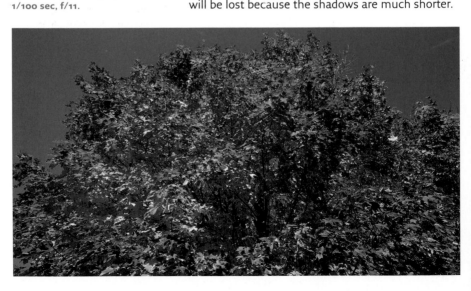

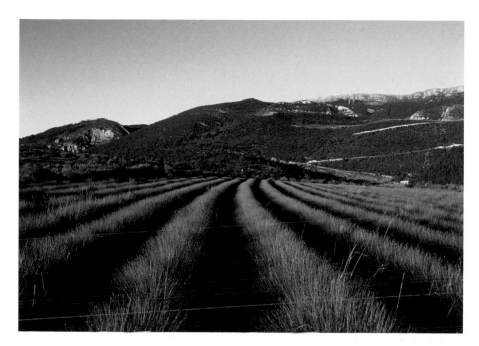

A telephoto lens is good for isolating detail, and either a macro lens or an extension tube will help you get in close for fine features, such as the veins of a leaf. In this case, you might want to try a shot from a low angle with the sun backlighting the leaf.

Without the early-morning sun, the furrows in this out-of-season Provençal lavender field would look flat and uninteresting.
> Canon EOS 1DS, 28mm lens, 1/6 sec, f/11.

Other autumnal themes

There are other features associated with autumn besides the changing foliage of trees. Pumpkins, for instance, are increasingly popular at this time of year, primarily because of their connection with Halloween. They present the photographer with a variety of shooting possibilities – their colour, size and texture can all be utilized to great effect. To accentuate the texture, it's a good idea to use strong side lighting to form deep shadows in the ridges of the pumpkin's skin.

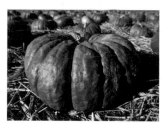

Early-morning light creates strong shadow detail in this pumpkin. To emphasize it, I used a telephoto lens. An aperture of f/16 ensured the other pumpkins were visible.
> Canon EOS 1DS, 200mm lens, 1/60 sec, f/16.

Winter

Winter is a great opportunity for shooting snow pictures, and a DSLR also gives you the scope to photograph distant wildlife with a telephoto lens or details with a macro. Although a compact digital camera might also offer these options, it will never provide the range of lens alternatives of a DSLR system.

Snow readings

Where there is a lot of snow, it can be difficult to determine exposures accurately, especially with the camera's built-in exposure meter. This is because with so many bright and reflective surfaces, the meter may think that there is more light than there actually is, which could result in your shots coming out underexposed. When you start shooting, keep an eye on the camera's LCD screen for the first few

Snow details can look better than an expansive view. The snow is in striking contrast to the deep blue sky, while the dark rock and the strong sun define its texture well.
> Canon EOS 1DS MK2, 150mm lens, 1/1000 sec, f/8, 100 ISO.

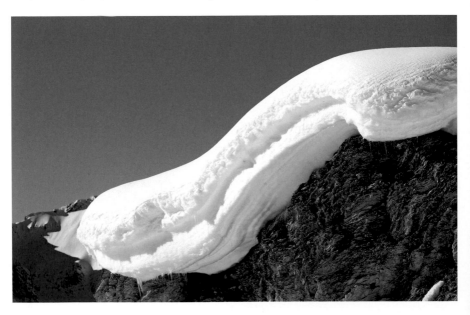

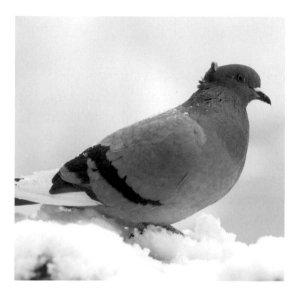

must know

• Camera batteries may seize up if they get too cold. Carry a couple of spares and store them next to your body to keep them warm.
• If your camera gets covered in snow, blow it off immediately rather than wiping it away.

The only way to get close to a bird in a situation like this is to shoot with a telephoto – here, a 300m lens. However, with a lens this length or longer, it is essential that you use a tripod or at least a monopod.
> Canon EOS 1DS MK2, 300mm lens, 1/50 sec, f/5.6.

shots and pay particular attention to the histogram. This will give you an accurate indication as to whether the meter is performing correctly.

Timing

The best pictures are usually taken immediately after it has finished snowing, when the trees are weighed down with snow and the sun is out (but see the daffodil picture, right). If there is no shadow detail and the skies are leaden, snow scenes can easily look uninteresting. A strong blue sky, on the other hand, provides colour, as do wild flowers and berries or a brightly coloured sign, and relieves the monotony of endless stretches of virgin snow with little or no shadow detail.

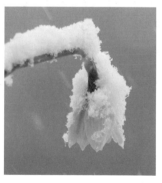

The layer of snow on this daffodil provides strong colour contrast to the background. The streaks of falling snow, captured with a slow shutter speed, break up the grey.
> Canon EOS 1DS MK2, 200mm lens, 1/30 sec, f/5.6.

Spring

Unlike winter, which can sometimes feel endless, spring can, if you're not careful, be over before you realize it. One minute, the trees are bare and flowers are a rarity; the next, the trees are covered in leaves and flowers are everywhere.

Planning ahead

Spring flowers, unfortunately, won't last for ever, so all the more reason to make sure that you know where and when they will be in bloom: daffodils, for example, are at their peak for only a few days. Plan ahead if you need to shoot in an unfamiliar area, and when you arrive, try to enlist the help of local knowledge to prevent wasting time and getting lost.

A field of oil seed rape contrasts with the new leaves on the trees and blue sky. A graduated ND (neutral density) filter has balanced the exposure required for the sky with the foreground, retaining the detail in the clouds.
> Canon EOS 1DS MK2, 40mm lens, 1/100 sec, f/8.

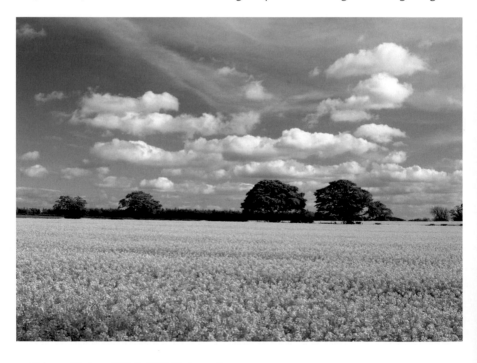

Close-ups

When taking close-ups of flowers, use a telephoto and perhaps an extension tube to allow you to get in really close to your subject, while keeping a physical distance. This is important because if you are too close to your subject, you or your camera might cast a shadow over it. Alternatively, use a macro lens: a 100mm macro lens, for example, allows you to magnify your subject without getting physically close to it, which would be impossible with a 50mm lens.

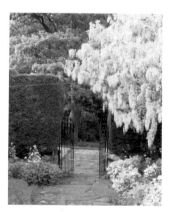

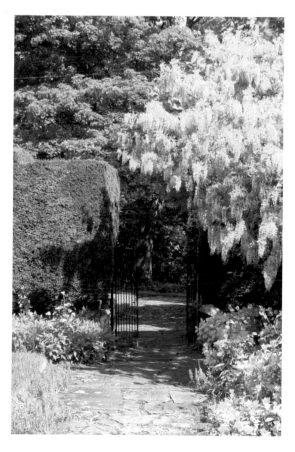

Although clouds had obscured the sun, conditions were still bright enough to take this shot (above). However, it looks flat and uninteresting. Look at the difference the sun makes (right). Everything looks brighter, while the shadow detail on the path adds depth and gives the background more interest.
> Canon EOS 1DS, 70mm lens, 1/30 sec, f/16.

Water

Shooting water in all its various forms – rivers, waterfalls, lakes, oceans – provides endless opportunities for great imagery, but being well prepared in terms of equipment and its protection goes a long way in ensuring the success of your photographs.

Safety first

DSLR cameras and water don't mix, so it's a good idea to take a few initial precautions before setting off on a shoot, especially if you are going to be by the sea. I always keep each lens and also the camera body in individual plastic bags to shield them from the wet, even if I'm carrying them in a backpack or camera case as well. The bags also protect them from sand, which gets everywhere and is particularly destructive: sand on a lens can

The shutter speed for this shot was only 1/20 sec as I used a polarizing filter, which requires up to two stops more exposure than normal. A small aperture let me create the greatest depth of field and maintain sharpness from foreground to horizon.
> Canon EOS 1DS MK2, 17mm lens, 1/20 sec, f/22.

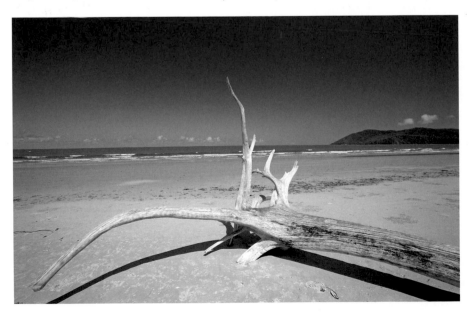

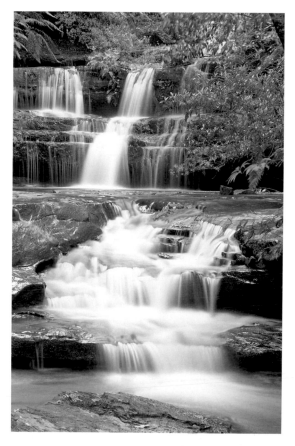

To give the impression of fast-flowing water, I chose a shutter speed of 8 seconds. A tripod was essential for such a slow speed and meant I could take the shot from the middle of the river without worrying about getting the camera wet.
> Canon EOS 1DS, 55mm lens, 8 secs, f/22.

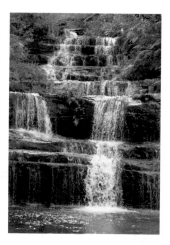

For this version of the same scene, I used a shutter speed of 1/250 sec to virtually 'freeze' the flow of the water. The shot is acceptable but not as dynamic.
> Canon EOS 1DS, 70mm lens, 1/250 sec, f/2.8.

ruin the front element within seconds. Another way to protect your lenses is to fit each one with a UV, or skylight, filter. These cost only a few pounds to replace, unlike a lens, which can cost thousands of pounds. If, in spite of all your precautions, a lens does get wet, wipe it immediately with a soft, dry cloth to remove all visible signs of moisture.

Dropping the lens and/or camera body into water will probably be the end of them. Even if they could be repaired, the cost of doing so is likely to be prohibitive, so do be careful.

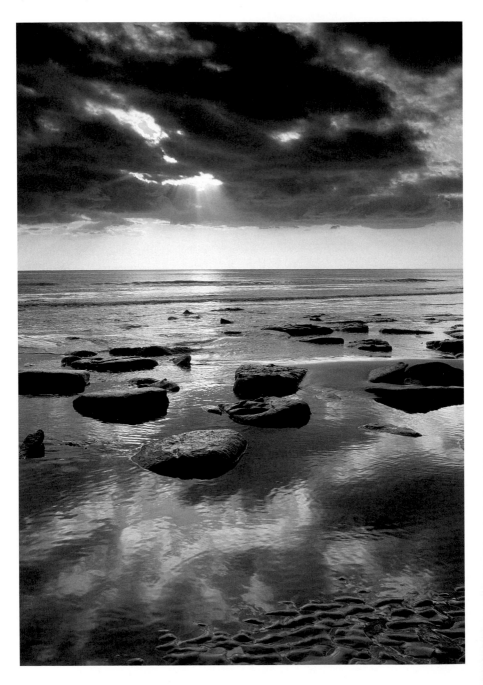

Using a tripod

When shooting fast-flowing water, you might want to use a slow shutter speed to 'blur' the water. To do so, you will need to keep the camera completely still. Even though you might be able to brace yourself against a tree or wall, or rest the camera on a rock, for example, the support might not be in the best position for your shot. This is when you need a tripod.

Filters and reflections

A polarizing filter is a particularly useful accessory when photographing water. Apart from darkening a blue sky and highlighting clouds, it will also change the appearance of the water. However, you need to use it with care if the reflections in the water, such as clouds, overhanging branches or mountains, are an important part of your picture because one of the other functions of the polarizing filter is to eliminate reflections. In this case, you might be better off using a graduated ND (neutral density) filter, which will balance the exposure required for the sky with that of the foreground without affecting the quality of the water.

Sunrise and sunset

If you are shooting a sunrise or sunset over water, it will be best to use the K setting of your camera's white balance. Having the camera set to AWB (auto white balance) could neutralize the warmth in the sky, which is probably the reason why you are taking the picture in the first place. As with so many controls on DSLR cameras, there is a time and place to use them in their auto mode, but getting to grips with the manual settings will give you far more

must know

- At sunrise, water is generally calm with mirror-like reflections. Later in the day, the water will ripple, making reflections disappear.
- A polarizing filter intensifies the blue of the sky and gives greater clarity to clouds.
- If using a wide-angle lens, don't include uninteresting detail in the foreground, 'pushing' the background so far away it is difficult to read any detail.
- Set the white balance to K for shooting late in the day or at sunset.

Opposite: For this sunset, I set the camera's white balance at K to retain the warmth and detail of the sky. A graduated ND (neutral density) filter also helped to accentuate the cloud details.
> Canon EOS 1DS, 24mm lens, 1/4 sec, f/11.

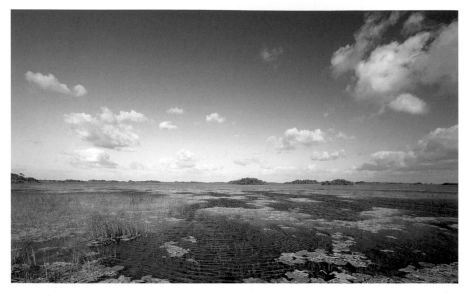

Using an ultra wide-angle lens, taking a low viewpoint and pointing the camera downwards to emphasize the foreground have worked well for this shot. The wind has created an intriguing ripple effect in the water, which could have looked quite 'dead' without any movement.
> Canon EOS 1DS, 17mm lens, 1/320 sec, f/5.6.

creative control over your shots. The advantage of digital over film, after all, is that you can review the results instantly on the camera's LCD, so do try to make full use of this.

Foreground interest

When composing pictures of large areas of water, think carefully about the foreground – nothing is worse than a vast area of water, sand or grass in the foreground of the picture with no interesting features to break it up. Always be on the lookout for a point of interest, which could be anything from a boat or unusual foliage to a piece of driftwood. If such a feature is at hand, think about where you are going to place it in the frame and vary the composition from shot to shot. You don't want to end up with a series of pictures that always feature the foreground interest in the bottom right-hand corner, for example.

Urban landscapes

While most people associate landscape photography with the countryside, there is another way landscape can be interpreted and that is through the built environment. As the majority of the world's population now live in cities, these tend to be a rich source of photographic opportunities.

Precautions

Towns and cities can be challenging to photograph, but a DSLR system is so flexible with the range of lenses and accessories available that you'll be able to shoot in almost any situation. The system is also quite light and not particularly bulky, so that you can carry a reasonable amount of kit comfortably

From this high viewpoint in Rio de Janeiro, the beach umbrellas look as though they have taken up every centimetre of space.
> Canon EOS 1DS, 80mm lens, 1/250 sec, f/11.

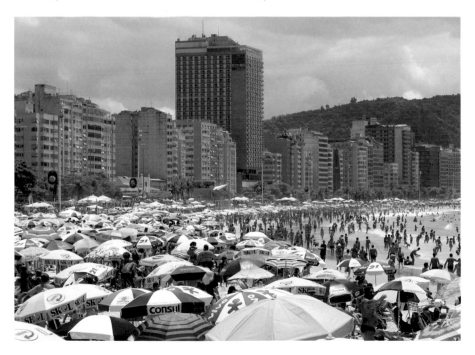

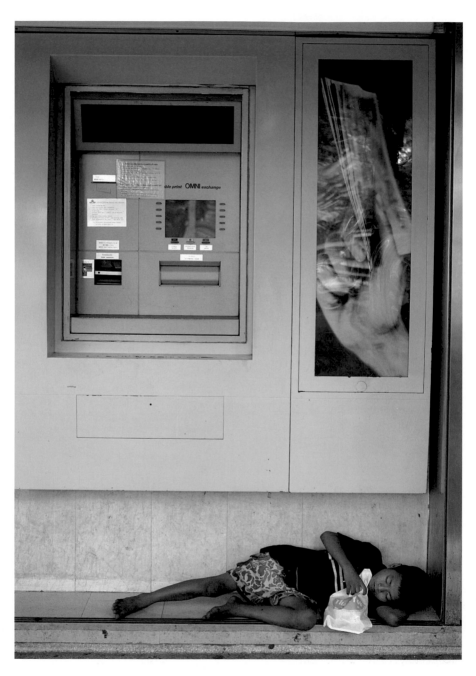

without getting in people's way. However, shooting with a lot of expensive kit on show could make you a target for robbery. I've found, though, that having my camera on a tripod and appearing familiar with my surroundings can work to my advantage. People assume that I'm a professional and probably not working alone. In addition, there is a limited market for selling stolen professional kit, whereas a more modest camera is easier to dispose of.

Choosing the ISO

One of the great advantages of a DSLR is that you do not need different speeds of film in order to change the ISO. I find that either 100 or 200 ISO is suitable for most situations. However, if the light is low, I can increase the ISO to suit. Even at 800 ISO, the results are amazingly good and the level of noise is negligible. In any case, I would rather cope with noise than use flash, which could easily ruin the atmosphere of a shot.

Subject matter

When shooting urban landscapes I tend to focus on the detritus created by people living in close proximity to one another. This does not have to mean the obvious – piles of rubbish on street corners, although this can be interesting – but rather the way we clutter the environment with electricity cables, street signs, billboards, graffiti and so on. I never set out to portray the built environment as one of chaos and decay. After all, my home is in London, which I find a fascinating and vibrant place, as well as a source of beautiful architecture, both old and new.

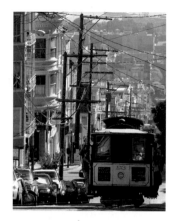

This jumbled environment of telegraph and electricity poles, parked cars and background buildings in San Francisco appears even more compressed through a telephoto lens.
> Canon EOS 1DS, 200mm lens, 1/400 sec, f/8.

Opposite: I found this young boy asleep in front of a Bangkok cash machine. In similar situations, I would usually discuss taking the photograph with the subject, rather than do it secretly.
> Canon EOS 1DS, 50mm lens, 1/125 sec, f/2.8.

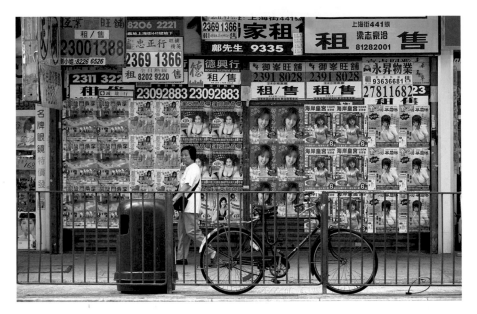

In any urban environment, as soon as a business closes down its frontage becomes covered in advertising posters. I took this colourful shot in Hong Kong.
> Canon EOS 1DS, 100mm lens, 1/250 sec, f/2.8.

Using colour

Colour plays a big part in the built environment, so I am always on the lookout for ways I can use it in my shots, unlike many photographers who tend to shoot in black-and-white as a way of portraying the negative aspects of city life. Remember that if you shoot in colour, you can always convert your images to black-and-white at a later stage on the computer, thereby giving you the best of both worlds. If you shoot in black-and-white, though, you won't be able to convert it to colour.

Lenses for urban photography

I have a tendency to favour longer lenses over wide-angle ones for urban photography, although that doesn't mean I don't include one of the latter in my kit. With a longer lens, I find that I can fill the frame and create the illusion of bringing the background

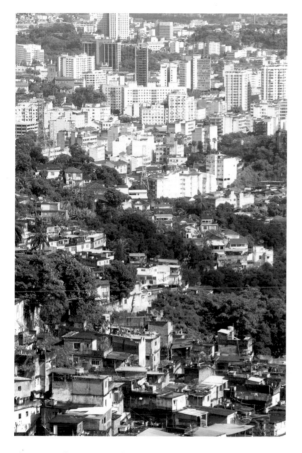

I chose a medium telephoto lens to show the two contrasting sides of housing in Rio de Janeiro. It has brought the more affluent background closer, juxtaposing it with the *favela* in the foreground.
> Canon EOS 1DS MK2, 150mm lens, 1/160 sec, f/8.

closer and compressing the picture, so that the distance between the foreground and background appears reduced. I often use a 70-200mm lens for urban shots to give me flexibility, and sometimes I increase the maximum focal length to 400mm with a 2x extender, although this does mean that the maximum aperture is reduced from f/2.8 to f/5.6. The zoom lens and extender are much easier and lighter to carry around than an additional 400mm lens, which would definitely need a tripod in order to keep it steady.

want to know more?

- Walk if possible in big cities. You will see so much more on foot and you can stop easily to take a shot.
- Use maps to study the area beforehand and to find possible places of photographic interest.
- There are some useful websites you can visit for more ideas:
www.anseladams.com
www.outdoorphotographer.com

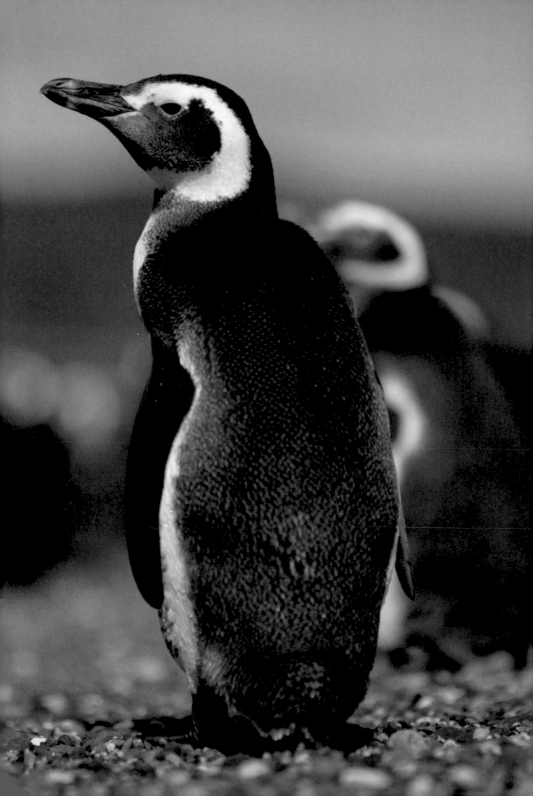

5 Nature

Wherever we live, we are surrounded by the natural world. Whether it is flowers and plants or animals – domestic or wild – you are never far away from a great photographic opportunity. The important point to remember is that nature is not going to wait for you, so you need to be prepared with the right kit and make sure that your batteries are fully charged!

Plants and flowers

Plants do not have to be exotic and rare to make great pictures; those growing in your own garden, window box or flower pot, even cut flowers from the florist, can create marvellous images. There are no hard-and-fast rules about equipment – the shots here were taken with lenses ranging from fisheye to telephoto.

must know

• Take care not to cast your own shadow over the subject when you are working close-up.
• Use an extension tube to get in closer than the normal closest focusing distance of your lens.
• Invest in a macro lens for life-size images.
• Look at the plant from all angles; don't be afraid to shoot into the light.

Shooting outdoors

There are certain points that you need to consider when shooting plants and flowers outdoors. You may want to stop the lens right down to get as much depth of field as possible. As this will mean a slower shutter speed, you might need a tripod. Even in a light wind, plants are unlikely to stay completely still for you, resulting in a blurred image. To 'freeze' this movement, the shutter speed may have to be at least 1/250 sec but this, in turn, may mean that you won't be able to stop down as much as you'd like, reducing your depth of field. This is not such a drawback as you might think. All lenses have an aperture that gives optimum sharpness but

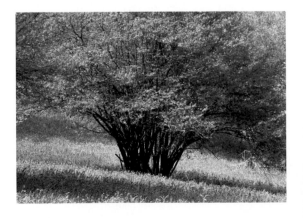

Look for large expanses of wild flowers, such as bluebells. Their lifespan is quite short, so take such shots at the earliest opportunity.
> Canon EOS 1DS MK2, 120mm lens, 1/50 sec, f/8.

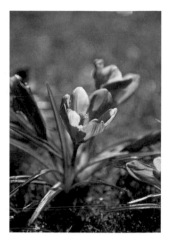

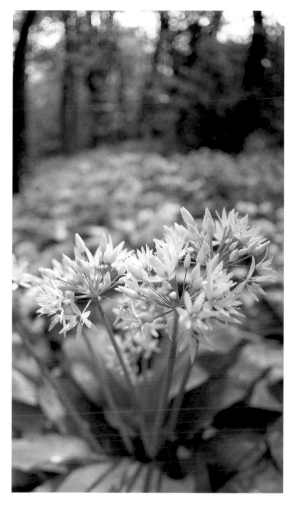

Above: Shooting this crocus with the sun backlighting the petals intensified their purple colour. The narrow depth of field was created using a telephoto lens combined with a wide aperture.
> Canon EOS 1DS MK2, 200mm lens, 1/400 sec, f/2.8.

I took this shot of wild garlic with a fisheye lens. You can just see the curvature created by the lens in the background. The flower was 10cm (4in) away from the lens.
> Canon EOS 1DS MK2, 15mm lens, 1/1650 sec, f/2.8.

this is not necessarily the smallest one available. The smaller the aperture, the more the light 'bends' as it passes through the lens, and the more it bends, the less sharp the shot. So, although there might be more overall in focus at smaller apertures – greater depth of field – the focus will not be as crisp at the point on which the lens is focused as it would at a wider aperture.

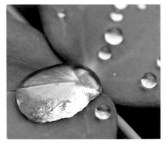

Other natural phenomena in plants, such as water droplets, add interest. To get in this close, I used a No. 2 extension tube between the camera and lens.
> Canon EOS 1DS MK2, 50mm lens, 1/50 sec, f/8.

I shot this in daylight coming through a window. A white reflector bounced light back onto the flowers. The shutter speed was slow, so I used a tripod.
> Canon EOS 1DS 200mm lens, f2/8

To get in really close to your subject, you will need either to fit an extension tube or use a macro lens, which enables you to focus close enough to provide life-size images. If you're planning to specialize in photographing plants and flowers, investing in both of these pieces of equipment will be worthwhile. Make sure you don't cast your own, or the camera's, shadow over the subject by choosing your viewpoint carefully. I prefer to shoot on bright but overcast days when the light is even and there are no shadows – on really sunny days, shadows are too harsh. Also, watch out for shadows cast by surrounding plants or flowers. You may need to bend them out of the way rather than alter your viewpoint.

Shooting with the sun behind a flower, when the light highlights the petals and creates an aura around them, might be beneficial. If you do this, you can either expose for the highlights of the petals, which will underexpose the background, or

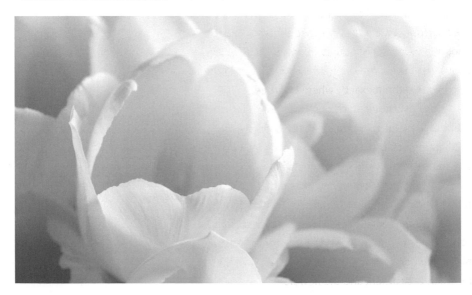

use a reflector to throw light back onto the flower. The reflector needs to be neutral, such as white or silver – a gold one will create a colour cast that will alter the colour of the flower. With backlighting, you need to be alert to light entering the lens, which can create flare. In some situations, though, this might be desirable, creating a romantic atmosphere.

Shooting indoors

Another way to photograph plants or flowers is to move them indoors and light them with available light or with flash. The white tulips opposite, for example, were lit with the sun coming in through a window behind them. Having chosen the viewpoint, I positioned a white card reflector between the camera and the tulips,and 'bounced' light back onto the flowers. This has created a very high key picture, which means that the tonal range is at the light end of the scale, with the focus centred on just the edge of one flower. I used a 70mm lens for this and set the aperture at f/8 with a 1/15 sec shutter speed. Shooting indoors meant that I didn't have to worry about the flowers moving in the wind, and I could also position them exactly where I wanted.

I always use studio flash to shoot flowers in artificial light – it gives me complete control over the lighting, which I can position and direct exactly as I please. To take the indoor shots shown on this page, I deliberately kept the light as diffused as possible. I fitted a softbox to the flash head, which emulates sunlight on a hazy day, and positioned it behind the flowers so that they were backlit. I then placed a white reflector on either side and another between the camera and the flowers.

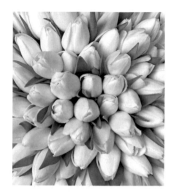

I had the florist arrange these tulips so they appeared to spread from the centre of the frame. I then placed them directly under the camera mounted on a tripod, and took the shot from above.
> Canon EOS 1DS, 24mm lens, 1/60 sec, f/16.

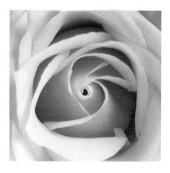

Flowers make exquisite close-up photos but need careful lighting. Ensure the petals do not cast ugly shadows over one another. The same goes for you and your kit.
> Canon EOS 1DS, 24mm lens, 1/60 sec, f/16.

Wild animals and birds

The DSLR system is so well served with a large selection of telephoto lenses that it is particularly suited to photographing wild animals. Even the most modest lens is capable of getting you in close to the biggest cat or the most timid bird.

Lenses and budget

Unless you specialize in wildlife photography, you are probably better off buying a modest telephoto lens, such as a 200mm, or a zoom lens that extends to 200mm. A 2x extender will increase the focal length to a maximum of 400mm, bringing animals several metres away close enough to fill the frame. Remember that with any extender you lose speed: an f/2.8 lens will become f/5.6, while an f/4 lens will become f/8. This is why I always recommend buying the fastest, albeit most expensive, lens that you can afford.

You need patience to photograph wild animals. I had set up my camera on a tripod and trained it on this alligator. After observing it for 20 minutes, it suddenly yawned, which made the shot.
> **Canon EOS 1DS, 250mm lens, 1/1250 sec, f/6.3.**

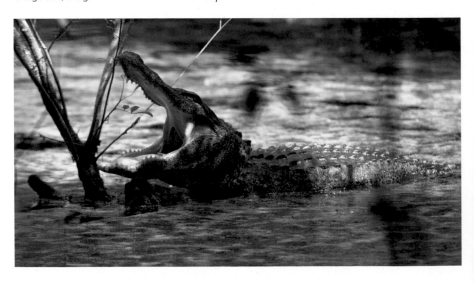

If you specialize in this type of photography, you might consider an ultra telephoto lens, such as a 400mm. They can be as fast as f/2.8, and the optics are superb. An extender can be added, so a 2x will give you a lens with a massive 800mm focal length.

There are two drawbacks, though, to lenses with such long focal lengths: the cost, which runs into thousands, and the weight. It is virtually impossible to hand-hold them steady, and you will either have to use a tripod or monopod – the latter should be adequate and is a much lighter option. The addition of such a lens to the rest of your kit will make it heavy and cumbersome. On a safari, you are likely to be in a four-wheel drive, but if you are trekking, it's unlikely you'll be able to cover a lot of ground.

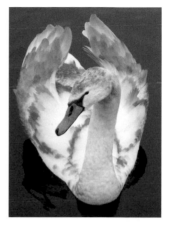

Even close to home wild animals and birds flourish. I photographed this cygnet not far from my home in London. This shows why it pays to always carry your camera .
> Canon EOS 1DS, 70mm lens, 1/250 sec, f/8.

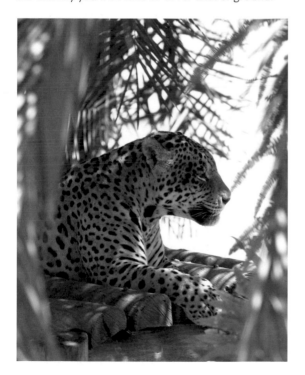

Although I used only a modest 200mm lens to photograph this leopard in a safari park, I was still able to get in close.
> Canon EOS 1DS, 200mm lens, 1/400 sec, f/4.

Pets and domestic animals

Photographing pets and domestic animals should be easier than shooting wildlife because you are more familiar with their habits and temperaments. You should also be able to move in closer.

Automatic programs

All animals can be unpredictable, so, in order not to be caught unawares, set your camera to one of its automatic programs, such as shutter priority, which allows you to select the shutter speed while the camera automatically sets the aperture. This way you can concentrate on the animal's movements without worrying that you have the correct settings. If there is not enough light, even when the camera chooses the widest aperture, you will either have to select a slower shutter speed or increase the ISO to

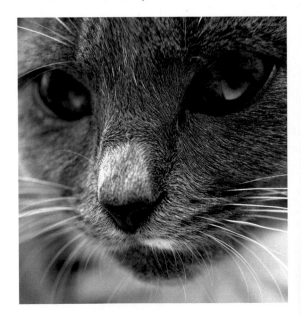

To get in close to this cat without upsetting her, I used a No. 2 extension tube. Being so close has reduced the depth of field, so only half the face is in focus.
> Canon EOS 1DS MK2, 70mm lens, 1/100 sec, f/5.6.

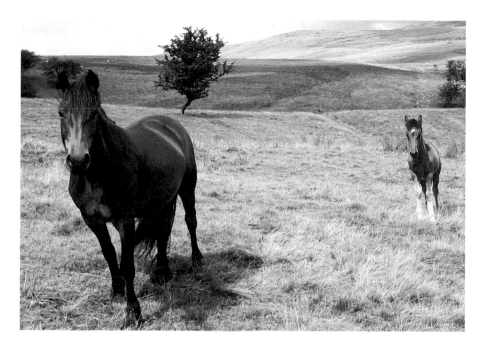

Take care when photographing animals with their young. This mare was very wary of me and kept her foal at a distance.
> Canon EOS 1DS, 150mm lens, 1/250 sec, f/8.

a higher rating. Whenever I have the camera set to one of its auto modes, I always do a small series of test shots first – it may be necessary to fine tune what the camera predicts and have to use the compensation adjustment, 1/3 of a stop either over or under.

Lenses and light

I usually use my 24-70mm zoom lens to photograph pets and domestic animals, so I can get in close to the subject or pull back for a wider shot. It also works very well with extension tubes, which allow me to get in even closer. I prefer to work in available light, and avoid flash as much as possible because it can upset animals, making them more unpredictable than usual.

want to know more?

- Zoos and wildlife parks provide us with different animals to photograph. Most of us live within easy reach of these.
- Flower shows are popular in the summer months and provide us with a wide range of unusual plants to shoot.
- Look on the Internet for websites that specialize in natural history. Log on to: www.heatherangel.co.uk

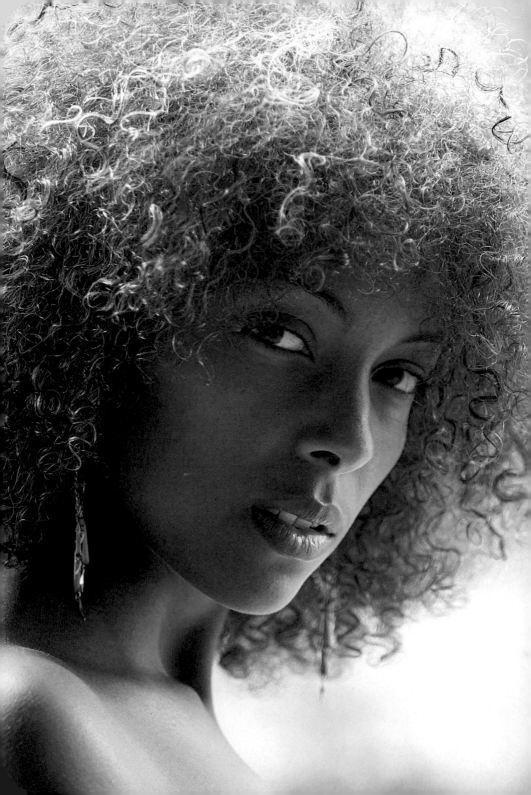

6 People

Pictures of family and friends are the subjects that dominate most people's photographic ambitions. This is hardly surprising, as we have been making representations of one another since cave times. Using a DSLR gives you the flexibility of choosing different lenses, controlling backgrounds by using depth of field effectively and reviewing your shots instantly on the camera's display, so that perfect portraits can be shot every time.

Portraits: outdoors

The human face and body are probably the most popular subject for photographers. Although the majority of outdoor portraits will be of people you know, you'll probably also shoot complete strangers, especially if you are travelling abroad.

must know

- Using a low viewpoint for a full-length portrait makes legs look longer, which is more flattering.
- Shooting from a low viewpoint with a wide-angle lens exaggerates leg length even more, but the head may appear unusually small.
- For posed outdoor shots, put a concealer for blemishes in your kit.

Useful kit

A medium telephoto lens – anything between 70 and 200mm – is ideal for outdoor portraits, whether they are headshots or full-length portraits. With it, you can get in close and fill the frame and, if you are using a wide aperture, you can put the background

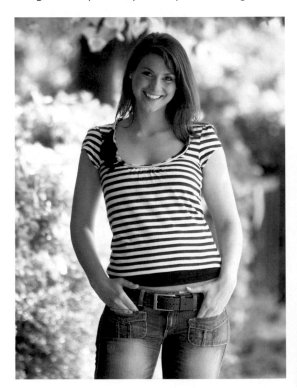

Although a 400mm telephoto lens combined with a wide aperture may seem an extreme choice for a portrait, it has produced a flattering shot with a bright yet muted background. I used a monopod to help support the weight of the camera and lens.
> Canon EOS 1DS MK2, 400mm lens, 1/50 sec, f/5.6.

out of focus, too, so that the emphasis is firmly on your subject. For candid shots, a 200mm lens is the perfect choice.

You can take excellent portraits with lenses of other focal lengths but it is only by experimenting with a range of different lenses that you will arrive at a choice that suits your particular style of photography. Extension tubes are also useful. Combined with a 100–150mm lens, they enable you to get in really close but not physically close so that you risk casting your shadow over the subject. A reflector or flash gun allows you to direct light to the face, soften shadows that might be heavy around the eyes and under the nose and chin, and alter the quality of light by making it cooler or warmer. Of the two, I prefer the reflector, and always have one folded up in my kit bag. It has a silver side for a cool light and a gold side for a warmer effect. With flash, try not to overlight the subject, as the result will appear unnatural.

Positioning your subject

Daylight is not as easy to work in as you might think. One reason for this is that you can't move it like you can studio lights, so you need to position your subject very carefully. When you start shooting, take a good look at how the light is falling on the face and if there are any harsh shadows. If the contrast is too great, consider moving your subject to an area of overall shade, or turn them around so that they are backlit. Although backlit portraits can create an attractive halo of light on the hair, be careful that the light doesn't cause flare by shining directly into the lens – even a lens hood or shield

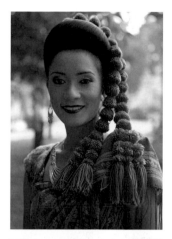

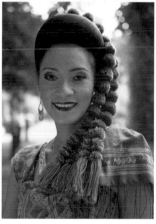

In this shot (top), the face of the traditional Thai dancer is in too much shadow and her costume looks rather dull. To rectify this, I asked her to hold a reflector silver side up and out of frame and angle it, so her costume was evenly lit and more colourful (above). The shadows lifted from her face, the skin tones are more pleasing and the reflector has been caught in her pupils.
> Canon EOS 1DS, 50mm lens, 1/320 sec, f/2.8.

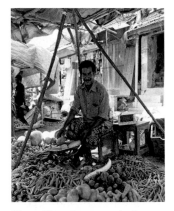

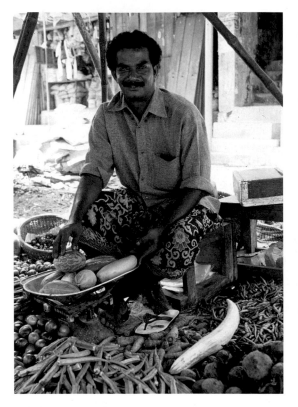

Above: There is too much clutter in this shot of a Madras market, such as the roof canopy and vendor in the background, and the framing could be improved.

Right: By zooming in, tightening the image, I cropped out the roof, background vendor and some foreground produce. My subject is now the centre of attention; he doesn't look so lost in the frame.
> Canon EOS 1DS, 50mm lens, 1/100 sec, f/8.

doesn't always prevent this. Shadows, such as those created by a parasol, can cause uneven illumination that will ruin your portrait. The solution may be as simple as moving your subject or changing your viewpoint slightly. If your subject is backlit, take your exposure reading for the shadow area.

Photographing strangers

In an unfamiliar place abroad, you may grab the first shot you can of a stranger and quickly move on, probably because you're unsure of their reaction to being photographed and too shy to ask for permission. Most people would be flattered, though, by such a request and be much more co-operative than if they catch you trying to photograph them unawares.

Calculating exposure

As DSLR cameras come with a built-in metering system, it should be quite easy to take a selective reading from the subject's face using the spot or partial metering method. Even though these systems are sophisticated, many professionals still use a hand-held meter for readings. With these you can use the incident light reading method, where you read the light falling on the subject, which is extremely accurate. A built-in metering system, on the other hand, calculates the exposure with the reflective light reading method, where you read the light reflecting off your subject, which is not so precise. Although there are accessories that fit over the camera's lens to emulate the incident light method, they are fiddly and time-consuming to use. Your money would be better spent on a modest hand-held meter.

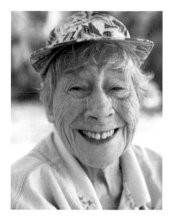

Sometimes a face is so strong it just has to be photographed. The muted colours of this woman's background and clothes help to highlight her features.
> Canon EOS 1DS, 50mm lens, 1/1000 sec, f/4.5.

Backlighting can produce a soft halo on the hair. I turned the subject so the late afternoon sun was directly behind her and used a white reflector to bounce light back onto her face, creating a very evenly lit portrait.
> Canon EOS 1DS, 200mm lens, 1/125 sec, f/5.6.

Portraits: indoors

There are a range of different light sources for indoor portraits, including available daylight, flash, reflected light and candlelight. Experiment with them to discover what works best for you in different conditions and situations.

Available daylight

Window daylight is my favourite indoor light source for portraits because it produces the most natural effects. However, it is changeable and does need to be managed effectively, which takes practice.

If your subject is seated near a window, take time to observe the quality of the light coming into the room. If the light is harsh, you could diffuse it by

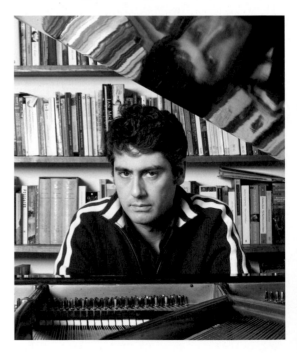

I kept the light coming through a window as directional as possible to create strong but acceptable shadows on one side of the face. Shooting in black-and-white meant that I didn't have to worry about colour casts caused by the very reflective piano cover.
> Canon EOS 1DS MK2, 70mm lens, 1/160 sec, f/2.8.

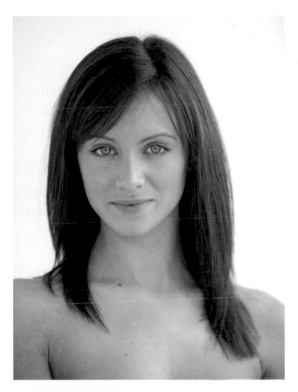

A window, covered with muslin to diffuse the light, formed the background in this shot. The addition of two reflectors either side of her face and another under the chin has resulted in a very soft, flattering portrait.
> Canon EOS 1DS MK2, 140mm lens, 1/40 sec, f/2.8.

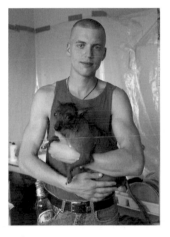

This portrait taken in a Moscow apartment was lit entirely with available light without reflectors. The pink-coloured wall to my right was light enough to soften the shadows and it also blended in with the man's flesh tones.
> Canon EOS 1DS MK2, 50mm lens, 1/30 sec, f/5.6.

covering the window with a translucent material such as muslin. This will even out the light and remove any strong shadows, but the light will still be directional. If the light is still too bright on the window side of the face, you can introduce a reflector to bounce light back into the shadows.

On the other hand, if the sun, even though bright, is not coming directly through the window, the light will be softer and without any harsh shadows. This is the type of indirect light that is favoured by painters, who refer to it as a 'north light' and have their studios built with, typically, a large, single window that faces north. Of course, for the southern hemisphere, the opposite is true.

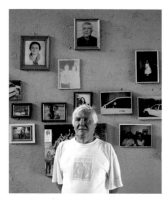

This man and the background had to be equally sharp because the wall was an integral part of the shot. I lit him with daylight and used a large white reflector to bounce light back into the shadows. As the light was still low, I rated the ISO at 1250.
> Canon EOS 1DS MK2, 35mm lens, 1/40 sec, f/2.8.

must know

• Use muslin, tracing paper or translucent material to soften the shadows when using daylight through a window.
• Select the camera's white balance (WB) carefully; avoid auto white balance (AWB), which can neutralize the ambience.

Reflectors

If the light is still too bright on the window side of the face, even with a translucent covering such as muslin at the window, introduce a reflector to bounce light back into the shadows. Look at your subject: the nearer you move the reflector to them, the more the shadows are reduced while the further away it is placed, the less it 'fills in' the shadows.

If you are shooting in colour, the reflector might create a colour cast, unless it is pure white or silver (the silver side gives a cooler light than the white), and you must adjust the white balance. Custom-made reflectors are portable and fold up into a small package. Normally they are supplied with a double-sided covering, so you have the choice of white and silver, or white and gold, or other reflective surfaces. You can make a reflector from a piece of white card or paper, a bed sheet, even kitchen foil stretched over a board. For a really soft light, you might want to use more than one reflector, perhaps positioning one to the side of the face and one under the chin.

Artificial light

For domestic tungsten lighting, you'll have to adjust the camera's white balance (WB), otherwise your shots will come out with a distinctly orange cast. Change the Kelvin (K) setting to 3500k or adjust the WB to AWB (auto white balance). Except in exceptional circumstances, I avoid the AWB setting because it can 'neutralize' the light to such an extent that all the ambience is lost. Whatever the setting, always check the LCD and the histogram.

The other common type of domestic lighting is fluorescent, which creates a greenish cast if the WB is set on daylight. There are so many different types of fluorescent light that it is impossible to set hard-and-fast rules about which setting to use.

Flash

Most beginners opt for flash if there is insufficient natural light. However, flash is never my first choice as most flashguns are too underpowered and the light produced is too harsh. However, if using flash is unavoidable, try to 'bounce' it off another surface, such as a white ceiling or wall. This creates a softer light than direct flash but can cause deep shadows in the eye sockets and under the chin. A flash gun with a smaller flash under the main flash to act as a fill-in helps eradicate this problem, although placing a small reflector under the chin at chest height does the job better. As with daylight, any reflector used with flash creates a colour cast unless it is pure white, so you will need to adjust the white balance.

Mixed lighting

If you are working with mixed lighting indoors, then choosing the WB can be problematic. You can rely on the camera's AWB or opt for the strongest light. If it's a choice between daylight and tungsten, work out which is the dominant source. If the daylight is the stronger, try to frame the shot tightly to reduce the area lit by tungsten light, which would come out with an orange cast. If you choose tungsten light and there is a window in the shot, this will come out blue. In either case, use these types of cast to your advantage and add warmth or coolness to your shot. If shooting in black-and-white, don't worry about the different colour temperatures of light.

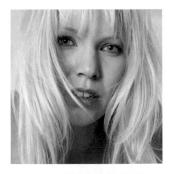

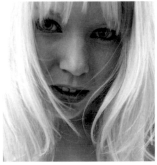

My first portrait (top) used flash and daylight. Although the shot is perfectly acceptable, the lighting is a little too hard. The second shot (above), taken in daylight with muslin at the window to soften the light, is more alluring. I exposed for the skin tones, slightly burning out the hair, but not to the detriment of the shot.
> Canon EOS 1DS MK2, 50mm lens, 1/60 sec, f/4.

Children: indoors

Getting children to relax in front of the camera requires great patience. If you are not prepared to spend the amount of time that might be necessary to achieve this, then you are not going to get the best and most natural shots.

must know

- **Photographing children in their own home relaxes them as they will be familiar with their surroundings.**
- **Toys can make useful props and also help to keep the child focused.**
- **If harsh shadows are created when shooting in natural light, diffuse the light by placing tracing paper, muslin or even a net curtain over the window to produce an even light.**

Planning your shots

Children are usually very lively and won't want to stay in one place for too long, so it's best to think ahead about the kind of shot that you want to take. For instance, if you are working with the available light, you will need to use as fast a shutter speed as possible to capture any movement that the child might make. Failure to do so might result in an unacceptably blurred picture.

To this end, you should think about increasing the ISO, which will enable you to work with a fast shutter speed. If you combine this with a fast lens and use the widest possible aperture, you should be able to shoot in any situation.

Natural and artificial light

When you are shooting in available light, do take time to observe it properly. If it is daylight coming in through a window, make sure that it is not too harsh and that the glazing bars, for example, don't create strong shadows.

If you are shooting in artificial light, such as tungsten, remember to set your camera's white balance accordingly. If you don't, all your shots will end up with an orange cast; in fluorescent light, they will have a green cast.

Flash photography

As mentioned on page 105, when using flash, think about bouncing it off a white surface, such as a ceiling or wall, instead of using direct flash. This will create a softer light, but make sure that it doesn't create dark shadows under the eyes and chin. Some flashguns have a small additional flash underneath the main one to act as a 'fill-in' for softening any shadows. Alternatively, you can place a small white reflector under the chin.

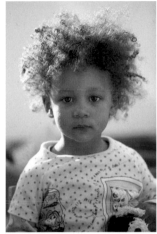

A wide aperture helps keep the background blurred, so the focus is on the child. The exposure was taken from the shadow side of the face. While the highlights are quite strong, they give a nice amount of modelling.
> Canon EOS 1DS MK2, 200mm lens, 1/200 sec, f/2.8, 100 ISO.

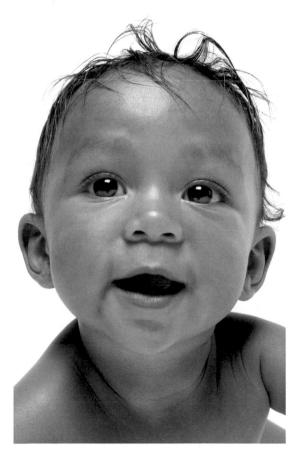

For this simple set-up, one flash was directed towards the white background and another, with a softbox attached, was fixed to a boom. This meant that I could work close to the light source but unhindered. I sat the child on a white sheet to bounce as much light back up as possible.
> Canon EOS 1DS, 70mm lens, 1/60 sec, f/22, 100 ISO.

Children: outdoors

As with photographing children indoors, shooting them outdoors in familiar places has some distinct advantages, but there are additional issues that have to be taken into consideration. Some of the information given for outdoor portraits is also applicable here, so please also refer to pages 100–103.

must know

- Children tire quickly, so photograph them as fast as you can.
- Using a low viewpoint to get down to the child's level can create very interesting shots.
- Break down older children's inhibitions by involving them in your photography, e.g. letting them hold your camera.
- A fast shutter speed will freeze movement, and a large aperture will blur the background to prevent distractions.

Working in sunlight

In familiar surroundings, children outdoors will quickly take up their favourite pursuits, such as climbing trees, and not be too concerned by you and your camera. Bright sunlight can be a problem, though, and you will need to keep an eye open for harsh shadows that might ruin an otherwise great shot. Once children are absorbed in whatever activity takes their fancy – and that probably won't be for long – take stock of the light. If the child is predominantly backlit, check whether the face is in too much shadow or the light is creating too much flare. If this is the case, decide whether you can move him without disrupting his play to an area that is more evenly lit. Alternatively, it might be best if you used a reflector or fill-in flash.

Mottled light filtered through the branches of a tree can create attractive patterns and pools of light on the skin. However, if these pools are falling on the wrong part of the face, they can create ugly highlights. Of course, children are not going to keep still, so in a situation like this you will need to keep one eye on them and one on the light in order to get the best possible shot! The benefit of shooting with a DSLR is that you are looking at the children through the lens, so there can be no discrepancy between what you see in the viewfinder and what the lens sees, as is the case with a compact camera.

Reflectors

Backlight produces a pleasant halo of light in the hair, but if it is strong, your subject could come out as a silhouette or very dark. In such a situation, you can use a reflector to bounce light back onto the child's face. As it might be difficult to position the reflector in the right spot if the child is moving, it would be useful to have someone available to hold it for you. The effect produced by a reflector appears more natural than fill-in flash.

Candid shots

When shooting outdoors, a telephoto lens will help you to get in close without intimidating the child or making him feel self-conscious. By observing the child from a reasonable distance you'll be able to get candid rather than posed pictures. A 70–200mm lens is the perfect zoom for this type of photography.

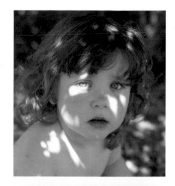

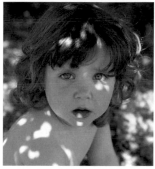

The mottled light falls in an unattractive way on the child's face (top), almost burning out the detail of her eye. By shifting to a slightly higher viewpoint and to the left, I've kept the mottled lighting but the pools of light fall in a more appealing way.
> Canon EOS 1DS, 70mm lens, 1/100 sec, f/5.

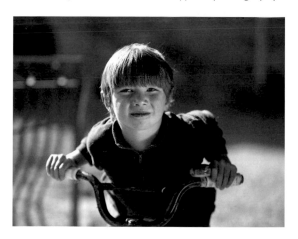

I chose to backlight this boy on his bicycle, which has resulted in a pleasant highlight on his hair. A white reflector has bounced light back into his face, creating two highlights in his eyes.
> Canon EOS 1DS MK2, 115mm lens, 1/640 sec, f/2.8.

Events

Few of us live such ascetic lives that we never take part in an event, perhaps a birthday party, wedding, carnival or religious festival. As a photographer, you will want to capture the essence of the event, its size, the people and the isolated details that make up the pleasure of the experience.

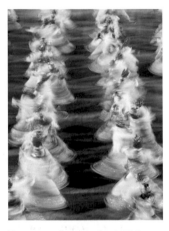

To convey the speed at which these dancers were moving, I found somewhere I could brace the camera and used a very slow shutter speed. I checked regularly to ensure the shots weren't so blurred as to be unreadable.
> Canon EOS 1DS MK2, 150mm lens, 1/12 sec, f/11.

Be prepared

For a large public event, such as a carnival or music festival, first of all consider your security. Keep all the kit that you are not using securely hidden away. This is especially true if you are using a backpack. If you can, fasten the zips with a lock. Alternatively, wear the backpack on your chest, so that you can keep an eye on it at all times. Worn in this way, the pack also gives you ready access to additional lenses and equipment that you might need. If you're shooting with a long lens, you're hardly likely to set up a tripod in the middle of hundreds of people, so use the backpack as a brace and rest for the camera.

At huge public events, I am always on the lookout for some candid pictures. This policeman deep in thought makes an excellent contrast with the back of the soldier in his bearskin.
> Canon EOS 1DS MK2, 150mm lens, 1/400 sec, f/2.8.

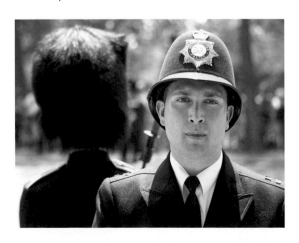

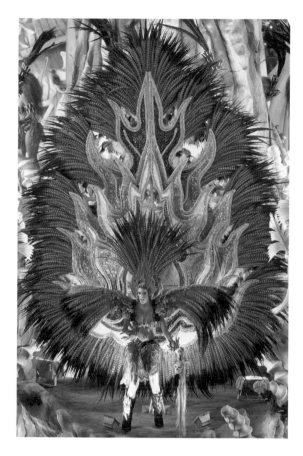

To compensate for the low light levels for this night-time shot of the carnival, I rated the ISO at 400. With a 200mm lens, I could get in close and fill the frame with a shot vibrant with colour.
> Canon EOS 1DS MK2, 200mm lens, 1/50 sec, f/2.8.

Capturing the moment

I am always on the lookout for the spectacular – something to fill the frame with a blaze of colour and really sum up the extravagance of the event. I tend to take such shots with a telephoto lens, which allows me to get in close and fill the frame. Being jostled in the crowd is inevitable, which makes a lens with an image stabilization facility a distinct advantage. Since many carnivals happen at night, you can always increase the ISO to a higher rating to compensate for the low light levels, or open up the

Make sure that you have a good position and are prepared for the finale – here a flypast of aircraft with coloured smoke trails over The Mall in London. You will get only one chance.
> Canon EOS 1DS MK2, 24mm lens, 1/320 sec, f/11.

At weddings, I always try to find a different angle from everyone else for my shots. I noticed the official photographer taking a shot of the bride and groom, and thought his body language lent humour to the event.
> Canon EOS 1DS, 70mm lens, 1/60 sec, f/5.

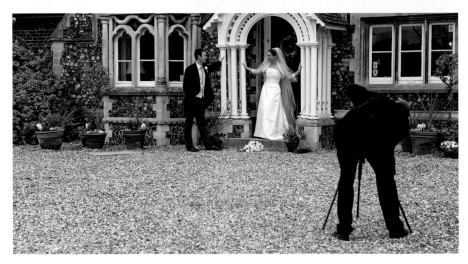

aperture so that you can increase the shutter speed. An interesting face in the crowd – usually someone who is completely absorbed in the whole experience – is another attraction for me. Depending on how close you are to the action, a medium telephoto is probably the best for this kind of shot, although I have had excellent results with a wide-angle lens. With a carnival, for example, much of the action takes place so quickly that you need to be on the alert, but as one float or troupe usually follows a similar route to another, you can generally be prepared and in position when your subject matter passes by. For the candid shot, you also need to be ready to shoot in an instant. Make the most of the crowd, letting it give you a certain amount of cover, so that your subject is totally unaware of your photographing them.

Formal events

There is generally an official photographer at most formal events like weddings, which can work to your advantage – as a guest, you'll be able to take pictures that they wouldn't consider. Distance yourself from official photographers – they have a job to do and it's important not to get in their way, but also there's no point taking the same shots as them. Look for the different angle and viewpoint. Remember that when official photographers are taking group pictures, they are probably doing it from eye level, so ask yourself what you could do from a high or low viewpoint. Observe the position from which other guests are taking their pictures and try to find the reverse angle. This can often result in unusual but very attractive shots.

want to know more?

• Always be on the look-out for possible models. Joining a local camera club may help you to find good models.
• Keep an eye on images used in magazines and study a various journals for inspirational ideas.
• Check the local press for news of events in your area. They may provide interesting shots of people.
• Specialist websites can be useful. Log on to: www.kodak.com

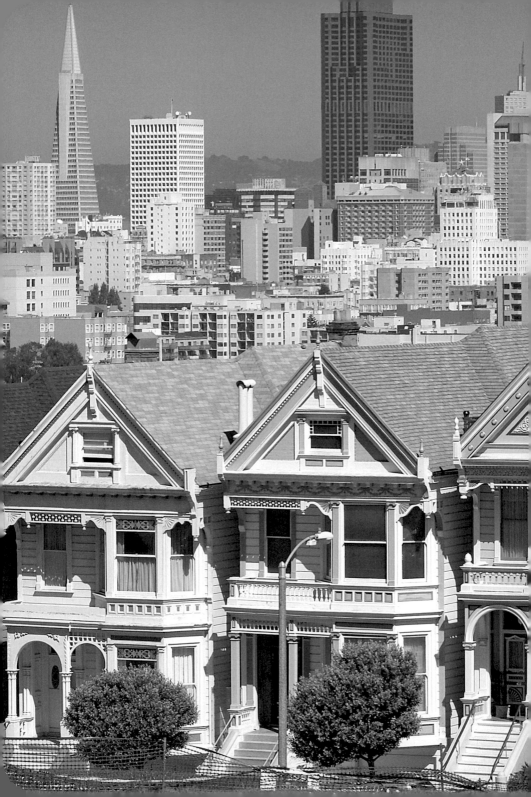

7 Architecture

Most DSLR cameras have a range of shift and tilt lenses in their arsenal. These are ideal for architectural photography when it is important to keep all the verticals straight, so that tall buildings do not look as though they are falling over. However, dynamic shots can also be created by using wide-angle lenses to increase perspective. The important point is to keep an open mind and experiment.

Buildings

Wherever we live, buildings form the common thread of our lives and existence. However, what makes them such a rich subject for photography is their diversity, not only from one country to another but also from one part of town to another.

Changing light

Many people tend to stop noticing local buildings that they walk past every day, assuming that they will always look the same. But, as a photographer, you know that the appearance of even the most familiar object alters according to the light: as the sun shifts its position on a daily basis, so the way in which the building is lit changes, too. Since most buildings are permanent fixtures, you have the opportunity of viewing them at different times of the day and through the various seasons. If you put off shooting a particular building on a particular day, you cannot be sure that it will look the same the following week. On the other hand, you can

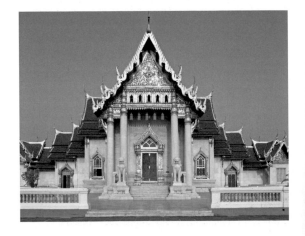

As well as the quality of the light, another reason for getting up early is to avoid people who can ruin your shots. I took this shot of a temple in Bangkok shortly after dawn, two hours before it was swarming with tourists.
> Canon EOS 1DS, 24mm lens, 1/320 sec, f/16.

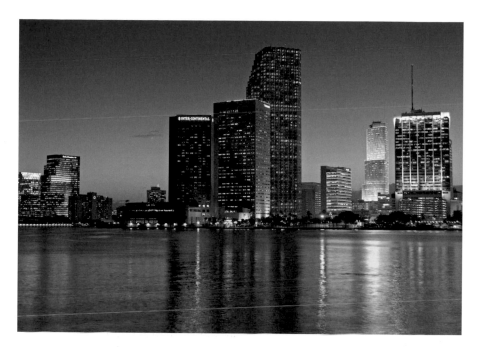

assess where the light might be at a later date and, weather permitting, plan your shoot for the time when the light is at its optimum.

Compressing distance

With a DSLR, you have the advantage of choosing from a wide range of lenses, which gives you great flexibility when shooting buildings. The picture of San Francisco on page 114 shows what can be done with a 200mm telephoto lens. I chose my viewpoint in the original part of the city and framed it so the old terrace of buildings was firmly in the foreground, with the financial district, or downtown, in the background. The distance between these two districts is probably about 9–11 km (6–7 miles), but the lens, in compressing the picture, has created the illusion that they are much closer together.

The twilight hour – about half an hour after sunset and lasting for 20 minutes – is my favourite time for photographing buildings at night. Any later and the skies are too black, reproducing with an unattractive heaviness.
> Canon EOS 1DS MK2, 80mm lens, 1/40 sec, f/11.

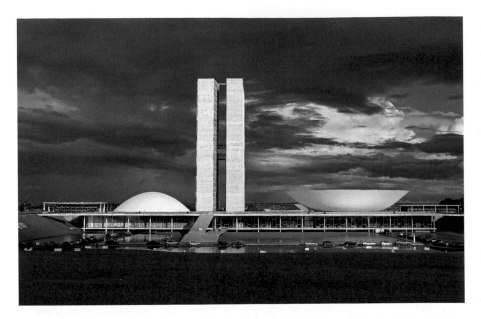

Directional sunlight and wild skies can enhance a shot, but you'll need quick reactions. The parliament building in Brasilia was soon in shadow as the storm clouds obscured the sun.
> Canon EOS 1DS MK2, 40mm lens, 1/500 sec, f/8.

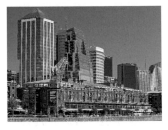

To sum up Buenos Aires' growing modernity, I used these tall, modern buildings as a backdrop to the old, low-level warehouses.
> Canon EOS 1DS MK2, 24mm lens, 1/125 sec, f/8.

Remember, however, that even a slight haze will be magnified by a telephoto lens, resulting in quite a murky background.

Converging verticals

There are occasions when the only way to get all of a tall building in the frame is to tilt the camera upwards, but then the building starts to taper towards the top. This effect is known as converging verticals, which are even more apparent with a wide-angle lens. Converging verticals can add dynamism to shots of modern buildings but if it's an effect that you would like to avoid, use a shift lens to include the entire building and keep all the verticals true.

A shift lens is also useful if you are photographing a highly reflective building where you and your tripod are clearly visible in the shot. By moving to one side so that you are no longer reflected, you can use the shift facility in its horizontal mode to bring the building back to the centre of the frame but without you appearing in it.

Avoiding flare

Modern buildings that are highly reflective can cause flare to enter the lens, especially on bright days when the sun reflects back from the metal or glass surface. Normally a good lens hood or shade will prevent this, but if it persists, change your viewpoint. Explore all the possibilities rather than let flare ruin the shot, especially as a suitable new viewpoint may be only a short distance away.

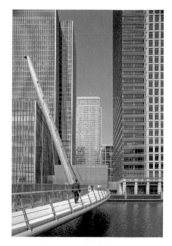

When shooting buildings, I try to find a viewpoint that sums up the environment. I chose this one in Canary Wharf, London, because I liked the way the curve of the bridge contrasted with the strong angularity of the buildings. Using a shift lens has removed the converging verticals.
> Canon EOS 1DS MK2, 24mm shift lens, 1/85 sec, f/22.

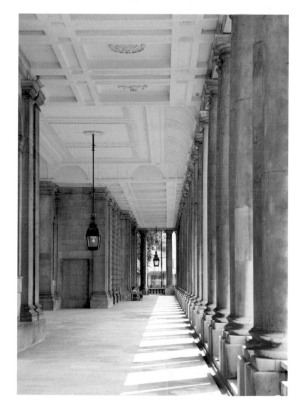

I wanted to emphasize this row of classical columns that forms part of the National Maritime Museum in Greenwich, London. I waited for the sun to move around the building so it shone through the columns, casting long shadows. This helped to give the picture depth, and added interest to the diffused lighting.
> Canon EOS 1DS MK2, 70mm lens, 1/250 sec, f/5.

Interiors

Photographing interiors can be one of the most challenging subjects that you tackle with your DSLR, but don't let that put you off because it can also be one of the most rewarding.

Ideal light

The challenge is in making the most of the lighting you have with you and balancing it with the types of illumination already present, such as daylight, fluorescent, tungsten and flash, even candlelight.

Probably the easiest type of light to work in when shooting interiors is available light, but this is not without problems. Imagine shooting the interior of a church with your viewpoint looking straight down the aisle. On a bright day, the sun may shine through the windows on one side of the church, drenching one half of the interior in harsh pools of light, while the opposite side is in shadow. Take these shots on a bright but overcast day, so the sunlight is diffused and the interior more evenly lit. Alternatively, wait until midday to see whether the sun will be directly overhead, with both sides of the interior evenly lit.

Colour balance

If the interior is lit by tungsten light, check if it needs supplementing with flash – this is necessary for large areas of shadow. If the light is even, set the WB (white balance) to 3400 Kelvins (K) or choose the tungsten setting from the WB menu. In either case, do a test shot and make any adjustments to the WB setting. If the exposure required is going to be a long one, select the long exposure setting.

Fluorescent light

Fluorescent light can be difficult to work with because there are so many different types of tube – white, warm white, cool, daylight and so on – that getting the right colour balance can be difficult. As with any interior photography, I would take a test shot and either have the WB on the fluorescent setting from the menu or use the AWB (automatic white balance). However, I have always found that while the AWB gives an adequate assessment of the correct colour balance, I always have to tweak it using the K setting.

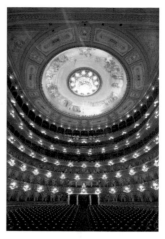

To light the interior of this theatre, I used every available house light. After several tests, I set the WB to 3550k, and selected a long exposure and the mirror up mode from the menu.
> Canon EOS 1DS MK2, 17mm lens, 5.2 secs, f/5.6.

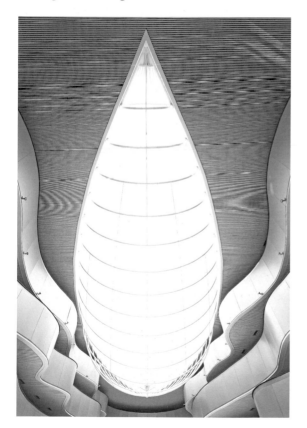

For this unusual view of the atrium of the Blue Trees hotel in Brasilia, with three levels of floor extending up the sides of the shot, I used a 17mm wide-angle lens. As the tungsten light was minimal, I used the available daylight as the source.
> Canon EOS 1DS MK2, 17mm lens, 1/6 sec, f/6.5.

Using flash

When photographing stained glass, the most important light is that behind the glass, giving you the detail. If the light outside is not as bright as the light inside, the window will come out underexposed and without any detail. Only use flash if you want to see the surrounding detail of the room. The calculation needs to be a perfect balance between ambient light – what is coming through the window – and flash – what is lighting the interior.

Getting the right mix

When an interior is lit by various sources, the trick is to get the right mix of the different light sources, so there is no colour cast. Ascertain what will be the dominant light source. If, for example, the sources are daylight, tungsten and flash, I would probably go with the daylight, as flash and daylight have the

I took this shot with a hand-held camera while on an underground travelator. A slow shutter speed created a degree of blur that is visible to the sides of the tunnel. I balanced the camera to the fluorescent light source.
> Canon EOS 1DS, 17mm lens, 1/5 sec, f/2.8.

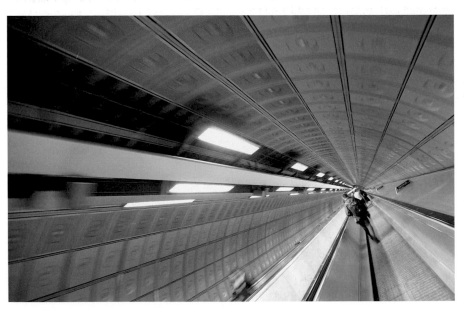

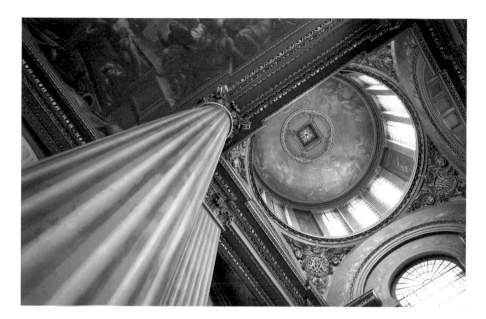

same colour balance, and set my WB accordingly. The tungsten might come out slightly warm, giving an orange cast, but this can add ambience. If it's too warm, you could use light balancing gels on the lights or change the bulbs to blue daylight balanced ones. If the dominant light source is tungsten and some fill in flash is all that's needed, cover the flash head with a light balancing gel to balance it to the tungsten. For a dominant fluorescent light source, use the appropriate green gel over the flash to balance it with the fluorescent light.

An interior may be so large it's impossible to add enough light to achieve the right colour balance. If the light is daylight filtering through stained glass windows, the chances are that the interior will be bathed in the predominant colour of the glass. Provided that this cast created the right ambience, I would accept it rather than not take the shot at all.

I try to find a different angle when photographing interiors. For this view of the Painted Hall in Greenwich, London, the pillar acts as a visual tool, leading the eye into the shot and adding drama to the composition.
> Canon EOS 1DS MK2, 24mm lens, 1/25 sec, f/2.8.

Architectural details

In addition to being shot in their entirety, buildings also lend themselves to being photographed in detail. Even the most minimalist modern building can make great photographs and form the basis for some stunning abstract shots.

Getting in close

Photographing details of buildings can mean going in quite close, but as the detail might be high up or inaccessible in the distance, a telephoto lens is an advantage. To keep the detail sharp, you may have to stop the lens down to achieve the maximum depth

Many modern buildings are covered with interesting details, such as pipes and ducting.
> Canon EOS 1DS, 58mm lens, 1/100 sec, f/2.8.

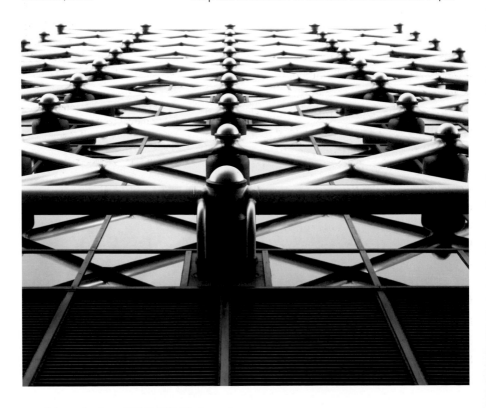

of field, although this doesn't necessarily mean your shot will have overall sharpness.

With a lens longer than 200mm, it's probably best to mount the camera on a tripod and use a cable release to prevent camera shake. This is especially true when shooting indoors with relatively low light that requires long exposures. To avoid having a very long exposure, you could increase the ISO setting instead. Depending on your camera, though, this could increase the noise to an unacceptable level, which, as you are photographing detail, could ruin the shot. In any case, it is wise to program your camera with the noise reduction facility.

Indoor light

Shooting detail inside a building means that you will need to consider the light carefully. In available daylight, you should check whether the light is too sharp, creating strong shadows that obscure some of the detail you are trying to bring out. Ask yourself whether it would be better to take the shot later in the day or to come back earlier on another day.

On the other hand, simply changing your viewpoint might alter the way the shadow is falling and be more acceptable. In artificial light, always make sure that you adjust the camera's WB (white balance) accordingly, so that your shots don't come out with a colour cast.

Composite images

Many shots of architectural details are perfect ingredients for making composite images using Photoshop or similar computer software. After downloading your image, you can then flip it to

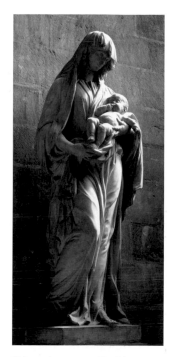

This sculpture was lit with daylight from a window high up to the right. It emphasizes the intimacy of the moment and spotlights the figure in gentle relief against the austere wall.
> Canon EOS 1DS MK2, 100mm lens, 1/400 sec, f/2.8.

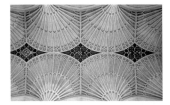

To make a composite image of the vaulted ceiling at Bath Abbey (above), I first downloaded the original image in Photoshop and made a duplicate, which I flipped and butted up to the original. I then kept on repeating the process until I had produced a kaleidoscopic effect (right).
> Canon EOS 1DS MK2, 28mm lens, 1/40 sec, f/2.8.

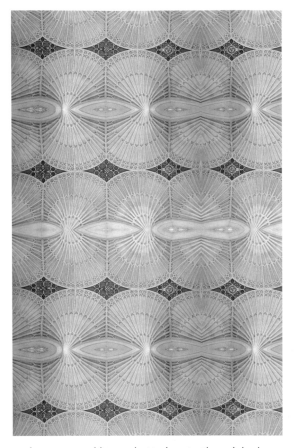

make a reversed image butted up to the original. You can then replicate this as many times as you like to produce an intriguing kaleidoscopic image for printing and framing.

You might want to make your composite out of several different shots with the same theme, such as doorways or tiles of a particular style that you have shot over a period of time. The more you put together into a single overall image, the greater the kaleidoscopic effect. If you have a collection of shots of various arches, you could use one of them

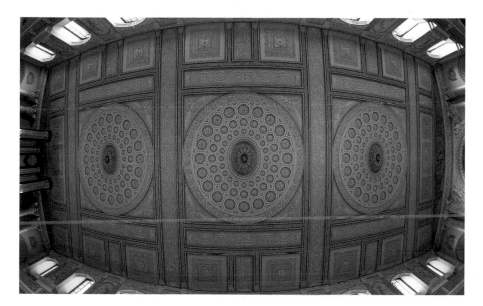

Fisheye lenses can create unusual ways of looking at the ordinary. Here, I managed to include the entire ceiling of this Wren chapel, and although it curves at the edges, this adds to the dynamics of the shot.
> Canon EOS 1DS, 15mm lens, 1/60 sec, f/5.6.

as the frame to a picture, with the view from another shot acting as the view through the frame. Such composites often produce a surreal effect and make the viewer look twice before realizing the deception.

Fisheye lens

Although it might seem a contradiction in terms because of its extreme angle of view, the fisheye lens can be used to great effect when you are shooting architectural details. It can create unusual ceiling patterns, for instance, especially in churches or cathedrals. A vaulted ceiling can look stunning and quite abstract when the entire expanse is included in the frame.

want to know more?

• Look at some specialist architectural magazines.
• Find out where the latest, most innovative buildings are located.
• Wherever you travel, there are always some interesting historical buildings to photograph.
• Open house events are good opportunities, as private buildings are opened up to the public. Log on to these websites:
www.riba.org
www.architecture.com
www.arcaid.co.uk

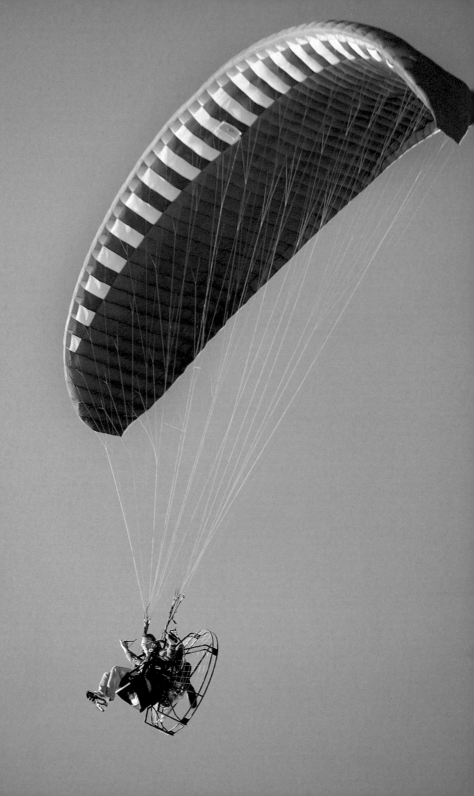

8 Action

Go to any sports event and take a glance at the kit the professional photographers are using. Without exception, they will be using DSLRs, together with a range of lenses – many ultra telephoto – motor drives and even radio transmitters for remote control photography. This should convince any sceptic of the scope of the DSLR system and how well suited it is to action photography.

Capturing the moment

If you go to any sports meeting, ranging from athletics to motor racing and winter sports, have a look at the cameras that the professionals are using – chances are they will all be DSLRs.

must know

- **Experiment first with all the different focusing modes on your DSLR to determine which one will best suit the event you are shooting.**
- **Blurred images can be effective at capturing a sense of speed.**

Why so popular?

Not only does the DSLR have a range of lenses ideally suited to action photography, but the rapid rate of firing means you can shoot a sequence of pictures without missing any of the action. In contrast, many compact cameras, especially at the low end of the range, have problems when shooting action.

Shooting speeds

The time that elapses between pressing the shutter release and the camera taking the picture is known as shutter lag. In some compacts this can be so slow that for a fast-moving sports shot the action could be over before the shutter fires, losing you the shot. At the top end of the DSLR range, this is not a problem because the picture is taken as soon as the shutter release is depressed. In addition, the motor drives in these cameras are extremely efficient: the Canon EOS 1DS MK2, for example, has a continuous shooting speed of approximately 4 shots per second.

DSLR cameras have a rapid buffering rate – the amount of time it takes the camera to write the image information to the compact flash card (memory card). If the buffering rate is slow, there will be only so many shots that you can take in rapid succession (bursts) before the camera won't let you take any more shots until the buffering is complete.

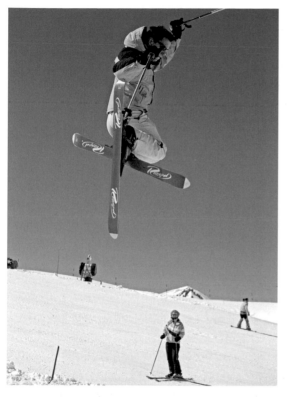

The best way to shoot movement is to see where most of the action takes place, then take up a safe position and wait for participants to come into your line of vision.
> Canon EOS 1DS MK2, 70mm lens, 1/2700 sec, f/5.

Not all shots have to freeze the action. I chose a slow shutter speed here and 'zoomed' the lens as I took the shot. The result is a car that looks as if it's moving at incredibly high speed.
> Canon EOS 1DS MK2, 170mm lens, 1/15 sec, f/20.

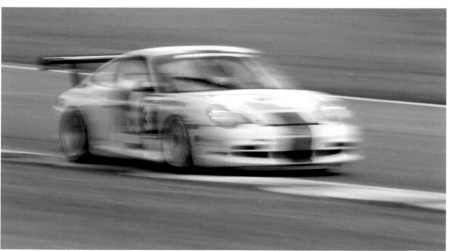

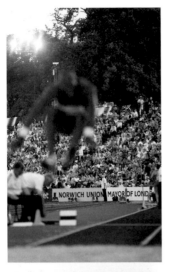

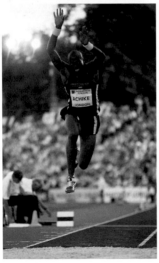

The maximum burst is also dependent on the size of file you are shooting and the type of compact flash card. If you save your images to the flash card as RAW files, the maximum burst will be less than if you save them as JPEGs because RAW files are bigger. With my Canon EOS 1DS MK2, the maximum burst with RAW files is about 11 frames, but with JPEGs I could capture up to 32 shots in one burst. I prefer shooting RAW because you get the greatest possible quality. RAW is like the negative in film photography – it has every scrap of information on it. JPEG is an interpretation of the information and as much as 20 per cent is discarded by the camera. Compact flash cards vary, too. The first 1GB cards I bought had a write speed of 16x, whereas on my latest 1GB card the speed is 133x. This means that the information is written so rapidly that I very rarely suffer from any delays in shooting action.

Focusing

DSLR cameras have different focusing modes. As well as manual focusing, which is where you focus the lens by hand, there is also the single shot mode, retaining the focus for as many shots as you like, and continuous auto-focusing, where the camera tracks the subject and constantly assesses the focus (AI Servo with Canon cameras). In sports photography or where the subject is coming rapidly towards you, this is a great asset, as the camera will keep the subject sharp, no matter how quickly it is moving.

Some DSLR lenses also have a predictive focus mode. Imagine you are opposite the goal at a football match. You could focus on this area and preset the focus, then concentrate on the action

Continuous auto-focusing can get the focus wrong if the sensor loses the subject (top). However, its accuracy is evident in the shot above, where the athlete is sharp against a blurred background.
> Canon EOS 1DS MK2, 200mm lens, 1/600 sec, f/2.8.

elsewhere on the field. When the action returns to the goalmouth, pressing the preset button makes the lens automatically reset the focus for that area. The advantage of this over auto-focus is if you are about to shoot the goalkeeper making a save but another player crosses your line of vision, the auto-focus can be distracted, and by the time it refocuses on the goalkeeper, the moment could have passed.

Lenses with IS (image stabilization) are an additional benefit when shooting action scenes with a hand-held camera. Any shake is detected by two built-in gyro sensors that then rectify the angle and speed of the camera shake.

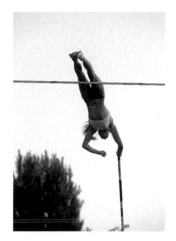

A shutter speed of 1/600 was fast enough to freeze the action of this pole vaulter with sharpness.
> Canon EOS 1DS MK2, 200mm lens, 1/600 sec, f/5.6.

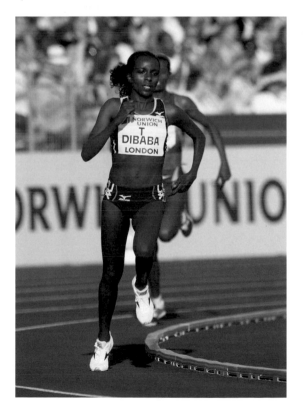

Using the predictive focus mode, I focused on this part of the track before the race began and logged it in the camera's memory, which left me free to shoot elsewhere as normal. As soon as the action returned to the predictive focus point, I pushed the PF button and the lens automatically refocused.
> Canon EOS 1DS MK2, 600mm lens, 1/800 sec, f/8.

Panning the camera

Although some DSLR cameras have shutters that fire as quickly as 1/8000 second, a very fast shutter speed does not necessarily produce the best action photographs. In some situations, you will find that panning the camera may be more effective.

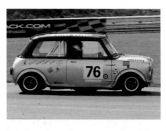

While a fast shutter speed might 'freeze' the action, it can take the drama out of a shot. Look at the wheels of this car – it is difficult to tell whether they are moving.
> Canon EOS 1DS MK2, 200mm lens, 1/800 sec, f/4.

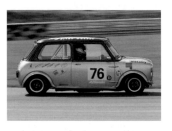

Choosing a slower shutter speed and panning the camera with the car has created a better sense of speed. The car is sharp but the wheels appear to be turning.
> Canon EOS 1DS MK2, 200mm lens, 1/60 sec, f/16.

Creating a sense of speed

The advantage of a camera with a range of different shutter speeds is that you can 'freeze' the action. In certain situations, this is desirable, even necessary, for a first-rate shot. However, it can ruin the appearance of some shots and erase any sense of speed.

For example, if you photograph a fast-moving car the moment it is directly in front of the lens with a shutter speed of 1/60 second, it will come out as a blurred streak with few of its features readable. On the other hand, if you were to increase the shutter speed to, say, 1/1000 second and take the shot when the car is directly in front of the lens, the camera will record the car perfectly and all of its detail will become visible. In this shot, though, it will be very difficult to tell whether the car is stationary or moving. In other words, any sense of speed or action will be lost and all that you will have captured is a static image of a car. The way to avoid this is to 'pan' the camera.

Panning is a term commonly used in the film world where the camera moves across a scene or tracks a moving object. In still photography, the technique is employed to give a sense of speed. It might take some practice but it is well worth the effort. Instead of using a fast shutter speed, you

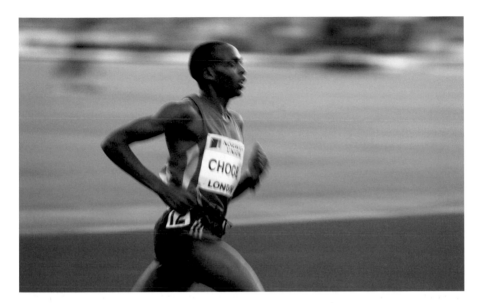

need to select one around 1/6o second. Point the camera to where the car is coming from and follow its path (pan) in the viewfinder. When it is directly in front of the lens, gently squeeze the shutter and take the shot, following through with the panning action in much the same way as a golfer does after hitting the ball. What you will have is a car that is sharp against a blurred background, giving a true sense of movement that is far more evocative than 'freezing' the action.

Vertical movement

Remember that a sharp and well-defined subject is possible only when the movement is along a horizontal plane, such as when a car is racing. If there is any vertical movement, such as the up and down action of an athlete's legs, these areas will not be sharp, although they will give an increased sense of speed.

This runner is moving on both a horizontal and vertical plane, so although the camera was panned with him, it was not possible to keep him pin sharp.
> Canon EOS 1DS MK2, 200mm lens, 1/6o sec, f/4.5.

want to know more?

● Find out where events will be held and look at the way the pros shoot.
● Take a camera on winter sports holidays.
● Go to indoor meetings of athletics and cycling events, to avoid weather problems.

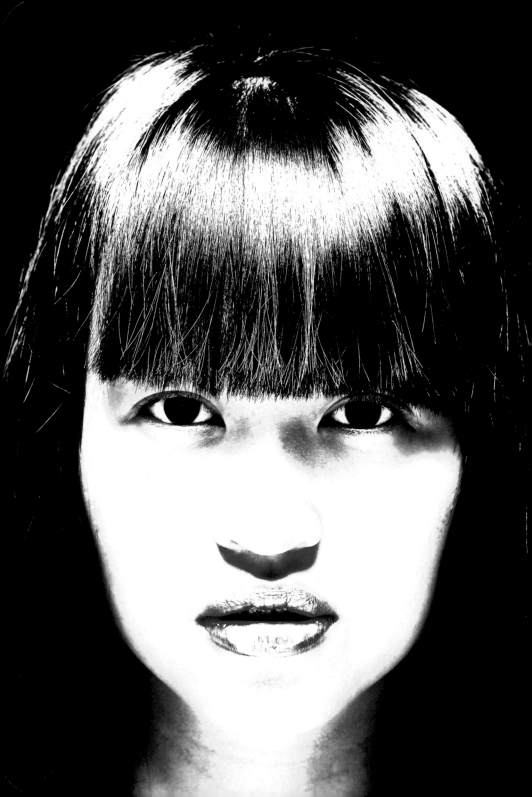

9 Getting more from your DSLR

Besides getting to grips with your basic kit, there many accessories that can make a difference to your DSLR photography. A polarizing filter can help your landscape photography by enhancing the blue of the sky and making clouds stand out with greater clarity. Extension tubes will allow you to get in really close, while flash and a simple reflector will improve your outdoor portrait photography.

Filters

If there is a drawback with digital photography, it is the tendency to leave everything to the computer and not to concentrate on getting the shot right in the first place. This is particularly true when it comes to using filters.

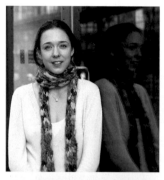

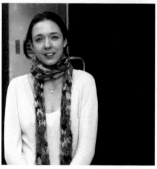

Polarizing filters are excellent for removing reflections. Without a filter, the girl and the building on the opposite side of the road are reflected in the glass (top). With a filter (above), the reflections have all but disappeared.
> Canon EOS 1DS MK2, 70mm lens, 1/40 sec, f/5.6.

Polarizing filters

Many photographers don't bother with filters at all, thinking that they can replicate their effects in post-production, but this isn't always wise. It is likely to lead to a build-up in work that will never get done and, when it comes to filters, the effects achieved in post-production will be a poor imitation of the real thing. This is especially true of the polarizing filter, which should be a permanent part of the DSLR kit.

Polarizing filters have several functions: darken blue skies and make clouds stand out with greater clarity; enhance the quality of water; and reduce reflections on shiny surfaces. There are two types of polarizing filter – circular and linear – but it is only the former that you should buy. (Your camera's auto-focus and metering systems will become ineffective with the linear polarizing filter, which is a pity because they are the cheapest to buy.)

For a polarizing filter to be really effective, you need to be careful about the time of day that you take your shots and the angle that you are to the sun. The best time is usually a couple of hours before and after midday, and it's important to keep the sun at right angles to the direction that you are shooting in. If you shoot with the sun directly behind you, the filter will have no effect at all on your images.

Be careful if using a polarizing filter with a wide-angle lens. As the filter is quite thick, it is easy for vignetting to occur, with the corners of the frame coming out dark. With lenses wider than 28mm, the effect of a polarizing filter will be uneven across the frame because the degree of polarization changes across the vista. Don't stop experimenting with this combination, though, especially as a DSLR allows you to see the effect directly through the viewfinder.

Once you've attached a polarizing filter to the lens and chosen your viewpoint, turn the filter (in effect, it is two filters on top of one another and the outer one revolves). As you continue to turn it, you will see the sky darken and then get lighter. The trick is to get the sky as dark as possible, then turn the filter back slightly to reduce the degree of polarization.

A polarizing filter can also change the colour of water and reduce reflections – however, this could have a detrimental effect on the overall composition if the reflections are a vital ingredient of the shot. Reducing reflections is useful when photographing objects with highly reflective surfaces, such as glass and metal. It is always important to remember that a polarizing filter will need approximately one and a half stops more exposure, so a tripod might be essential in certain circumstances .

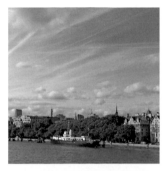

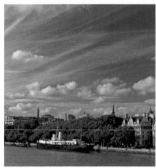

Polarizing filters are best known for the way they can enhance a sky. Without a filter, the sky (top) has a reasonable amount of definition but could be enhanced. With a polarizing filter (above), the clouds really stand out and the sky is a richer blue.
> Canon EOS 1DS, 50mm lens, 1/125 sec, f/11.

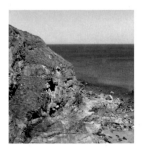

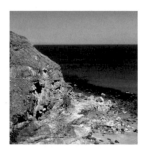

Far left: Although there's nothing actually wrong with this shot taken without a polarizing filter, it does look quite flat and plain. Left: Using a polarizing filter has improved the shot considerably: the sea has increased definition and the sky more depth.
> Canon EOS 1DS, 50mm lens, 1/60 sec, f/9.

Graduated neutral density filter

Also very useful is the graduated neutral density (ND) filter. Rectangular in shape, it slides into a special holder attached to the front of the lens. It is clear glass or plastic at the bottom, and then from halfway up looks like a band of grey coating. This grey coating comes in various strengths and cuts down the amount of light entering the lens without causing a colour cast. This means you can control different areas of your shot that require a different exposure, such as the sky and foreground. The difference in this case might be as much as one stop; if you don't correct it, the sky will be overexposed and without detail, or the foreground will be underexposed and also lack detail. As with the polarizing filter, you can see the effect as

Without a graduated ND filter this sky looks reasonable enough, and it would be possible, though time-consuming, to enhance it on the computer in Photoshop.

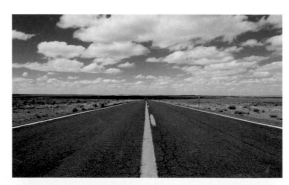

Using a filter improves the shot. Less exposure is given to the sky, preserving more detail, while the correct exposure is retained for the foreground.
> Canon EOS 1DS, 24 mm lens, 1/250 sec, f/11.

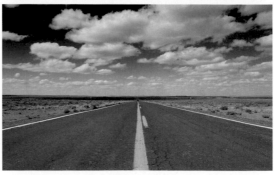

you look through the viewfinder, but you must take your meter reading before sliding the filter into position, otherwise your shot will be overexposed.

Filters for black-and-white photos

If you can shoot black-and-white images with your DSLR, you might find a set of filters useful: yellow to give greater clarity to clouds; red to darken blue skies; and green to lighten foliage and heighten features such as lips in portraits. However, if you shoot in black-and-white, you will not be able to change your pictures to colour later; if you shoot in colour as well, you will have both options covered.

If you shoot in black-and-white, certain filters will enhance your shots. The yellow No. 12 filter, used here, has given clarity to the sky.
> Fuji FinePix S2 Pro, 21mm lens, 1/60 sec, f/8.

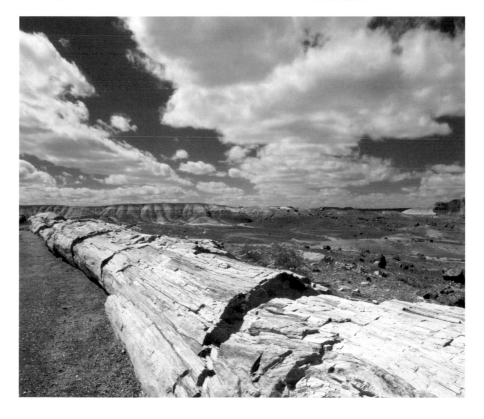

Fill-in flash

Using flash outdoors on a bright day may seem an anomaly but it can greatly improve the quality of your shots. So why would you want to use flash on a well-lit, sunny day?

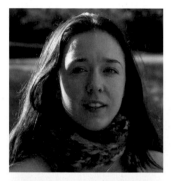

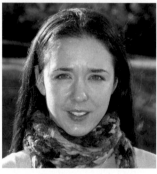

The sun was too bright to shoot this model facing the sun without her squinting, but positioning her with her back to the sun (top) has resulted in harsh shadows under the eyes and nose. To remove the shadows, I used fill-in flash but the amount that was fired in auto mode was too much, resulting in hot spots on the skin (above).

When to use fill-in flash

Fill-in flash is useful when bright sunlight causes unattractive shadows under the eyes and chin, and when your subject has their back to the sun and face in shadow. By using a small amount of fill-in flash, these shadows can be eliminated or softened. You can also use fill-in flash when your subject is in shadow but the background is in bright sun and you want to retain its detail. Expose for the background and the person will be underexposed and come out as a silhouette. However, expose for the person and the background will be overexposed and the detail burnt out. Instead of fill-in flash, use reflectors.

How to use fill-in flash

It is important to know how your flash performs. Practise and tailor it to this type of photography – many flash guns overexpose and give an unnatural appearance to portraits, often burning out detail and making the shot worse than it was originally.

To calculate the amount of fill-in flash to use, imagine that the daylight reading is 1/60 second at f/11. However, the subject is in shadow and the skin tones look dull. The camera is set to this exposure but the flash needs to be set to give half (1:2 ratio) of this exposure or even a quarter (1:4 ratio) – f/8 or f/5.6 respectively. In other words, there is less flash

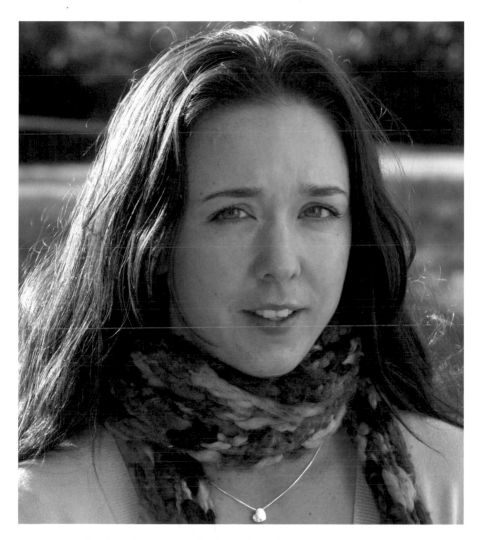

output than the daylight. The shot is then taken at f/11. With this combination, the surrounding areas are perfectly exposed and the amount of flash falling on the subject is just enough to brighten the shot and create a more flattering portrait. If your camera has built-in flash, this might not be possible and you will have to rely on its fill-in flash mode, if it has one.

To remove the hot spots, I set the flash to manual and cut its output by 1/4. This gave a more flattering portrait, with more detail in the hair and the face lifted out of shadow. You can just see the pinpoints of flash in the pupils.
> Canon EOS 1DS MK2, 155mm lens, 1/125 sec, f/11.

Reflectors

In photography, a reflector is anything that can 'bounce' light back onto your subject. Although often very inexpensive, they can make an enormous difference to your shots.

must know

• Small reflectors can easily be carried in a camera bag or pocket.
• Remember that the colour of the reflector will create a colour cast.
• Make a reflector from something as simple as a napkin or newspaper.
• Highly reflective surfaces can be as dazzling as the sun, so use them carefully.

Custom-made reflectors

There are many custom-made reflectors to choose from, starting at a cost of a few pounds through to several hundreds. Most come on an expandable metal or plastic frame, which either springs out into a circular shape with a diameter starting at about 300mm (12in) or into a rectangle that could be as large as 2 x 1.5m (6½ x 5ft). The frame is covered in a reflective material that is either white, silver or gold. Some custom reflectors come with a collapsible frame that slots together, with the reflective material stretched over it or attached with Velcro. Several of this type can be joined together to make a structure resembling an enormous tent.

Improvised reflectors

Not all reflectors have to be so elaborate, of course, and many can be improvised out of everyday items. At the beach, for example, a simple white towel could do the job just as adequately as a custom-made reflector. Remember, however, that if you were to use a light-coloured towel, perhaps a green one, then this would create a green cast on your subject's skin, which might not be quite the effect you had in mind. Another improvised reflector could be a newspaper, an open book, a white napkin or even a white piece of card.

When to use a reflector

A reflector is ideal when the sun is too bright for it to shine on your subject's face without making them squint and their eyes water. To remedy this, you could turn your subject so that their back is to the sun and then use the reflector to bounce light back onto the face. You can then direct the reflector to the area where you want more light.

For a head shot, it's often possible for the subject to hold the reflector. If you decide to use a highly reflective surface, such as gold or silver, remember that this can be as intense as the sun and could result in your subject screwing up their eyes. The further away you position the reflector, the less intense the effect.

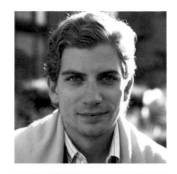

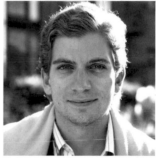

I was photographing this model outdoors on a bright sunny day. With his face to the sun, it was hard for him to keep his eyes open. Turning him around with his back to the sun, his face was slightly in shadow (top) and the lighting flat. I used a reflector with a white surface (above) to brighten the light on his face, but the effect is rather cool.

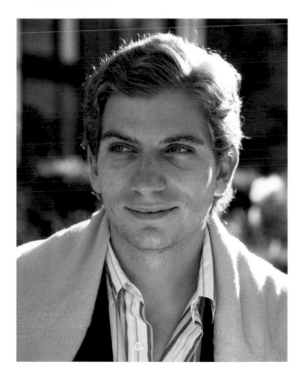

For the final shot, I used a gold reflector. This worked in the same way as the white reflector but added some warmth.
> Canon EOS 1DS MK2, 70mm lens, 1/125 sec, f/4.5.

Night photography

There are just as many photographic opportunities to be had at night as during the day, particularly in towns and cities when buildings and roads are lit up and headlights create light trails. There's also as much to shoot in winter as there is in summer.

Buildings can reflect beautifully in water at night, if you get the timing right. Here, the sky is just beginning to turn – any later and it would have been quite heavy, requiring more exposure and burning out the street lighting.
> Canon EOS 1DS MK2, 85mm lens, 5 secs, f/8.

The twilight hour

My favourite time to shoot cityscapes at night is during the twilight hour, which occurs about half an hour after sunset and, confusingly, lasts for about 20 minutes. If you want to take full advantage of this period, you need to be in position well in advance. I like this time because the sky turns a deep blue, which offsets illuminated buildings to best effect. After this time, the sky records as a deep black, which often looks too heavy and isolates buildings as blobs of light with little detail of their structure.

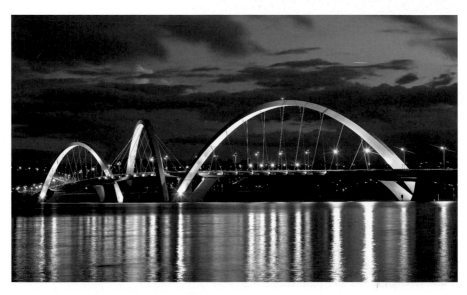

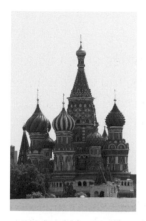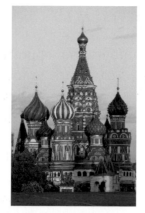

Far left: I took this shot of St Basil's Cathedral in Moscow in the mid-morning light, but knew it would look better at night.
> Canon EOS 1DS MK2, 180mm lens, 1/200 sec, f/8.

Left: I waited for the sun to sink until it hit the cathedral almost horizontally. The light was warm, which made the building look much more attractive than it did mid-morning.
> Canon EOS 1DS MK2, 160mm lens, 1/400 sec, f/4.

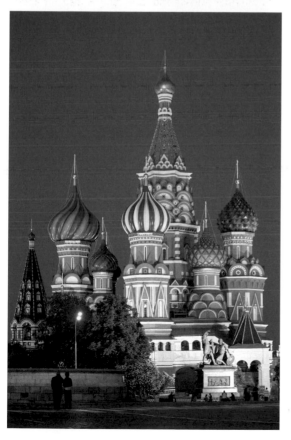

It was only at 10pm that night that I got the shot I wanted, but it was worth the 12-hour wait. The sky is a lovely twilight blue and the cathedral looks far more majestic than earlier in the day.
> Canon EOS 1DS MK2, 75mm lens, 1/4 sec, f/2.8.

Opposite: I try to photograph fireworks early on in a display before the sky becomes heavy with smoke, obscuring the detail. A tripod and cable release are essential for shots of fireworks.
> Canon EOS 1DS MK2, 70mm lens, 1 sec, f/8.

Equipment

A tripod is an essential piece of equipment for night photography, so your shots come out pin sharp. A good-quality tripod is definitely a very worthwhile investment, and will be useful for other applications besides night photography. You should also have a decent cable release.

Exposure times

Longer than normal exposure times are required at night. Many cameras have a shutter setting that is known as 'bulb', or 'B'. Set to this, the shutter will remain open for as long as the shutter release is pressed, but this can drain the battery quite rapidly, so always make sure that you have plenty of back-up. However, as many cameras now have shutter speeds of up to 30 seconds, you may never need to use this setting. Long exposures can create 'noise', giving a grainy look to images, which is especially obvious on large prints. Most cameras have a noise reduction, or long exposure, mode which you should set before you start shooting.

Keep an eye on your ISO setting. Increasing this to cut down on exposure time is common, and it can do the trick, but it can also increase the noise. As a rule, however, I would rather use a lower ISO and increase the exposure. Some DSLR cameras are better at reducing noise than others, and it is only by experimentation that you can determine the effectiveness of yours.

Once I have mounted the camera on a tripod and attached the cable release, I choose the 'mirror-up' mode from the camera's menu. This prevents the camera from vibrating at long exposures when the

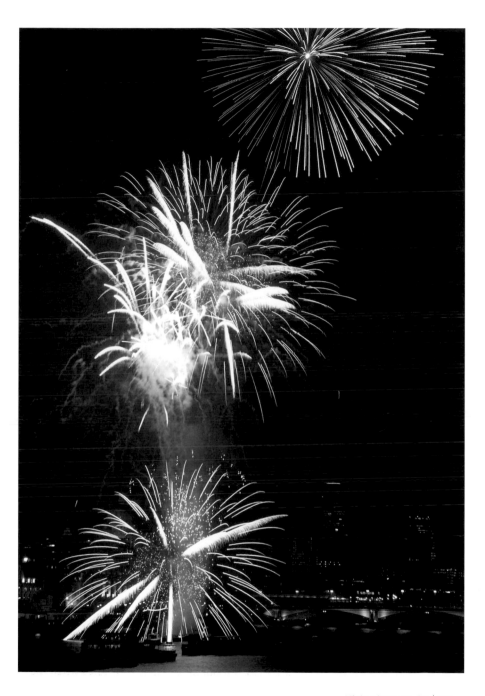

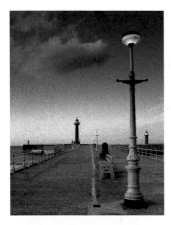

Evocative night pictures can be taken just after sunset. In this shot, the street lights were coming on, emphasizing that the day was over. The line of lamps creates a strong compositional element, while the red capstans add a splash of colour.
> Canon EOS 1DS, 50mm lens, 1/8 sec, f/5.6.

shutter is fired. In most cameras, this usually works on a double action procedure. When you have pushed the cable release halfway, the mirror goes up. Then you wait a few seconds, push the cable release further and the shutter fires.

Shooting options

Always try to shoot RAW if you can, so that you are able to adjust and improve your images later on the computer if you need to. If you shoot JPEGs, important information might be discarded as the camera interpolates the image.

Photographing fireworks

Fireworks are particularly worth shooting at night, but some forward planning is essential if you want a successful outcome. If you are familiar with the location of the display, make sure that you get in position an hour ahead of the first fireworks going off to be sure that your view won't be blocked.

Set the camera up on a tripod in such a way that people in the crowd won't kick the legs. As you will be at the front of the crowd, try putting two legs through any barrier, and place the third leg between yours. In this way, the tripod should be stable.

I usually work at 100 ISO and set the camera to 'B' with an aperture of about f/8. I focus the camera manually on a point below which the fireworks are going to explode. Once the display starts, I try to judge the frequency of the bursts and then open the shutter accordingly. As soon as there is a burst or two, I close the shutter. Fireworks soon turn the sky misty, so your best shots will be from the start of the display.

Close-ups

Taking close-ups can be incredibly rewarding for a photographer. Fortunately for us, the DSLR camera, with its enormous range of attachments, is perfectly suited to this field of photography.

How to get in close

There are several ways of photographing close-ups with a DSLR camera – with a macro lens; with extension tubes and bellows; or with a close-up lens that fits on the front of your lens like a filter. Although a close-up lens is the cheapest option, optically it is inferior to the lens you would be using with extension tubes or bellows, or a macro.

Macro lenses

Close-ups are best taken using a macro lens because they are specially made for this type of photography. However, beware that although many lenses are described as macro, they are not really – a true macro lens has the ability to photograph objects at life-size magnification.

As well as letting you get in close to your subject (approximately 30–60cm/1–2ft), a macro lens must allow you to shoot from a reasonable working distance. (f you need to get in any closer, you will have to combine your macro lens with an extension tube or bellows, see page 154.) For example, when photographing a nature subject, such as a spider, you wouldn't want to get in very close physically because you would disturb the creature, causing it to run off and hide. I would, therefore, recommend using a 180mm macro lens because it gives you a

must know

- Extension tubes are a more economical option than a macro lens.
- Always use a tripod and cable release.
- A 180mm macro lens will give you a greater working distance than, say, a 50mm macro lens.
- Don't cast a shadow over your subject.

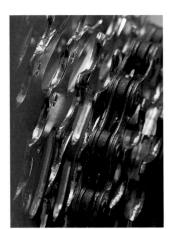

I shot these bicycle cogs using a macro lens. With my focus on the middle cog, it is easy to see how little depth of field there is when working this close to a subject.
> Canon EOS 1DS MK2, 180mm macro lens, 1/5 sec, f/11.

Opposite: Using a 180mm macro lens, I could keep a reasonable distance from this spider but still get in close. If the focal length of the lens had been shorter, I might have disturbed it and lost the shot.
> Canon EOS 1DS MK2, 180mm macro lens, 1/30 sec, f/8.

comfortable working distance as well as the ability to shoot life-size (with a shorter lens, such as a 50mm macro, your working distance for shooting life-size will be considerably reduced).

Keeping a maximum working distance from your subject is important for other reasons. If you are too close, there is always the chance that you could cast your own shadow over the subject. In addition, there might not be enough room for you to use a small reflector, additional lighting or a lens hood to prevent flare.

Some macro lenses come with a tripod mount, which enables you to move the camera quickly from a horizontal to a vertical position, and vice versa. This is important because if you change position with the pan-tilt head, you will alter the height of the camera and then have to adjust the tripod legs or its central column to compensate. In nature photography, this time lapse could be the difference between getting or failing to get the shot!

Extension tubes and bellows

Instead of a macro lens you can use extension tubes or bellows. Both fit between the lens and the camera body and enable you to get closer than normal to your subject. Their drawback is that they don't allow the lens to focus on infinity, so you have to remove them for normal photography.

Extension tubes come in a variety of sizes – the bigger the tube, for example 25mm as opposed to 12mm, the closer you will be able to focus. Two tubes can be joined together to obtain even greater magnification, but this will require an even greater increase in exposure. Extension tubes can be used

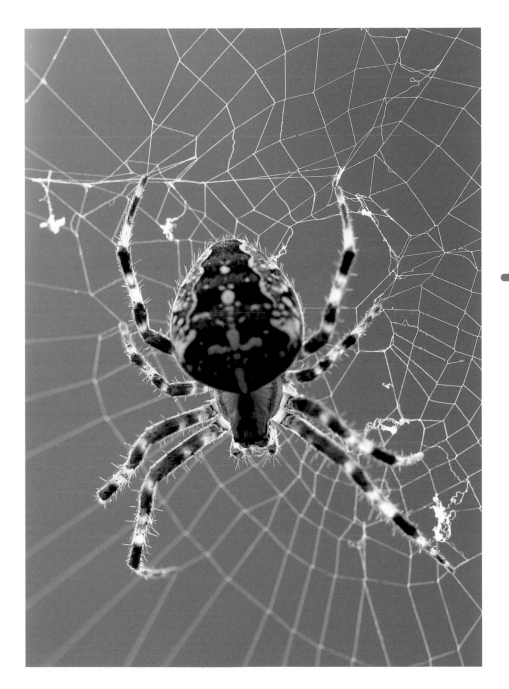

I shot this close-up of pencil shavings with studio flash as well as a No. 1 and a No. 2 extension tube doubled up. The front of the lens was only about 25mm (1in) away from the pencil shavings. A macro lens would have given me more working distance.
> Canon EOS 1DS MK2, 65mm macro lens + No. 1 and No. 2 extension tubes, 1/60 sec, f/8.

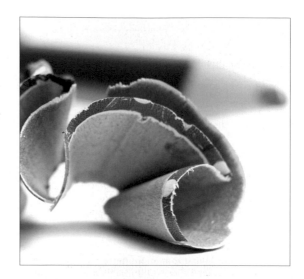

with many different lenses but are not compatible with fisheye and other ultra wide-angle lenses.

If you're thinking of doing a lot of close-up photography, you might want to consider buying extension bellows. These work in a similar fashion to extension tubes except that the magnification is variable, whereas with extension tubes it is fixed.

Focusing

Focusing is critical with close-up photography, and manual focusing is probably better than relying on auto-focus. This is because depth of field when shooting this close is minimal, and the A/F focusing point might have difficulty establishing a definite point on which to focus. A tripod and cable release are also advisable, as would be the use of the mirror-up facility and the self-timer.

When shooting close-ups, I focus, then depress the shutter release halfway, which sends the mirror up. I then press the release all the way. Alternatively,

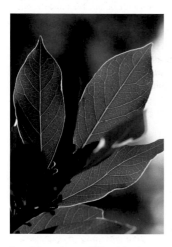

I positioned myself for this close-up of bay leaves so they were backlit by the sun. This emphasized the detail of the veins and their intricate pattern, which would have been lost if the shot had been lit from the front.
> Canon EOS 1DS MK2, 125mm lens + No. 1 extension tube, 1/30 sec, f/8.

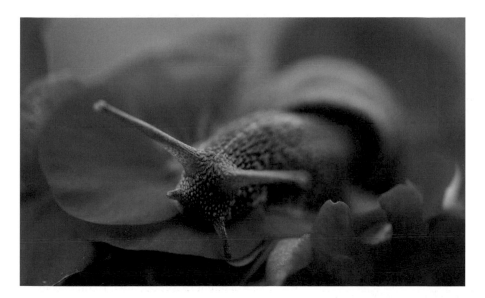

you can use the self-timer, which permits a reasonable amount of time to pass for the camera to settle and for any vibration that may have been caused by the shutter being fired to cease.

There is a tendency in close-up photography to stop the lens down as far as possible with the intention of increasing the sharpness of the shot. However, this is a fallacy because, although stopping the lens down might increase the depth of field, it won't increase the sharpness of the point on which the lens is focused. This is because light bends when it passes through the lens, and the smaller the aperture, the more the light bends.

A rule of thumb as to the optimum aperture for maximum sharpness is to stop down only three stops from the maximum widest aperture. Thus, a lens with a maximum aperture of f/2.8 will probably be at its sharpest when stopped down to f/8.

You don't realize how quickly snails can travel until you try to photograph one. This snail was quite compliant and didn't mind continually being repositioned.
> Canon EOS 1DS MK2, 180mm macro lens, 1/50 sec, f/4.5.

want to know more?

- Find the latest news on equipment in the photography magazines.
- Kew Gardens, London, have many exotic plants – take a look.
- Some useful websites: www.calumetphoto.co.uk www.canon.co.uk www.nikon.co.uk

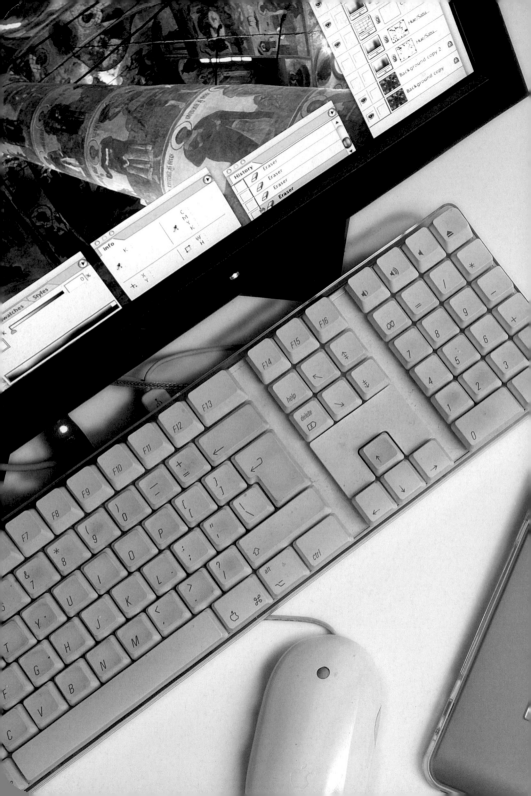

10 The digital darkroom

Having taken your shots you will need to
download them onto the computer. If you
have shot them as raw files they will need
to be processed in an image processing
programme. You will also need to back them
up in case your computer hard drive fails.
Once on the computer, there is a wealth of
options at your disposal with a programme
such as Adobe Photoshop.

Setting up a digital darkroom

The digital darkroom brings you out from the gloom into the daylight but it does need some key kit, including a fast computer with a good-quality screen, some image manipulation software and, at the very least, a printer.

The computer

The first thing you must get right is the computer, and there are some basics to look for. No matter whether you opt for an Apple Mac or a Windows PC, buy the one with the biggest screen you can afford. Go for the largest amount of hard disk space (the storage) and ditto for the amount of RAM – I would recommend a gigabyte (GB) RAM but definitely no less than 256 megabytes (MB). This is because you'll quickly find the hard drive filling up with the

A computer (here, an Apple Mac) that is ideal for image editing has plenty of hard disk space, lots of RAM and comes with a good-quality, large screen.

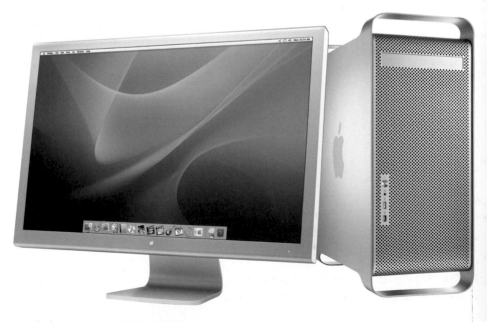

large images that modern DSLRs can make. Image editing software packages are memory-hungry beasts, needing lots of RAM to do their work. Too little RAM and you might find the programs running slowly or crashing on a regular basis.

Ideally, your computer should also have at least two USB ports (preferably the fast USB 2.0 system) and two FireWire (or IEEE 1394) ports to give you optimum communication speeds between devices.

The printer

Today's desktop inkjet printers can produce stunning photographs. They range in size from small, inexpensive, stand-alone printers producing 15 x 10cm (6 x 4in) prints to expensive A3 and larger printers. Many machines are combined printers, copiers, faxes and scanners, but all, bar the most basic (cheap) models, can still produce good prints. The advantage of buying an all-in-one model is you save on desk space without necessarily compromising on print quality. Some printers can bypass the computer and print directly from the memory card.

The printer manufacturer will recommend which paper and ink to use. These are generally their own brands, and they tend to be more expensive. However, this is not just a ploy to make you spend more money: the recommended ink and paper combination really does produce the best resuts.

Most inkjet printers use at least four, but as many as nine, inks together to achieve a good result. The four main colours are CMYK: cyan (C), magenta (M),

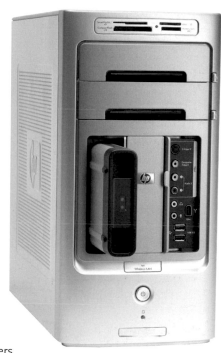

As well as having USB and FireWire ports, this HP computer has built-in memory card readers (at the top) so that you can plug a memory card directly into the computer to upload your shots.

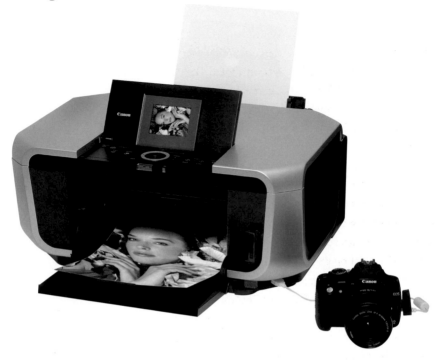

This inkjet printer has a built-in memory card reader and direct connection for a digital camera, making printing possible without an intervening computer.

yellow (Y) and black (K, which stands for 'key' and means the black ink). Additional inks can include light cyan and magenta to help with fine detail rendering, or red and purple to improve the range of colours that can be achieved on the print), while additional blacks and 'light blacks' are used for the same reason or to help improve black-and-white output. Generally speaking, the more inks there are, the better the output, but the more expensive the printer. To help keep costs down, try to buy a printer with separate ink tanks because, unlike printers with combined ink tanks, where more than one colour is built into a unit, you need replace only the tanks that are empty. As a rule of thumb, choose the highest-specified printer you can afford, but keep in mind the costs of the ink and paper.

The software

Image editing software is the final factor involved in producing great prints. Although with many DSLRs you can print directly from the camera without linking up to a computer, being able to access your images and manipulate them on the computer screen offers you a whole new world of creativity. The software ranges from inexpensive to very pricey, depending on how creative you want to be.

Your DSLR may come supplied with some form of image editing software – certainly, the camera should come with software to deal with RAW files. Adobe's Photoshop CS is one of the top-end very expensive image editing packages but Adobe also makes the much more affordable Photoshop Elements. Other packages include PaintShop Pro Photo XI, another Photoshop-like editing package. Again, this is much less expensive but it still has a full range of features and is very powerful.

The best course of action is to shop around and balance the level of skill you have (or don't have) with your budget, and if the software that was provided with your DSLR seems sophisticated enough for your purposes, then you need not spend any more money anyway.

Another useful gadget that can be enormously helpful with image manipulation is a graphics pad. Essentially, you 'draw' your edits on, and make changes to, your images with a pen-like stylus, instead of a computer mouse. Although this piece of equipment is relatively expensive, it does offer a more natural way of working than with a computer mouse, and you may well consider that it is worth the initial investment.

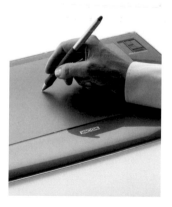

A graphics pad allows you to draw edits onto your images, which feels more natural and also gives you greater precision.

Basic colour management

You have a memory card full-to-bursting with images and now you want to print them. However, before you start, there are a few things that you can do to make sure that your prints will be of the highest possible quality.

Correct screen colour calibration is a critical first step to obtaining consistent colour across all your equipment and perfect prints.

Consistent colour

Colour management is simply a method of ensuring consistent colour on all your imaging tools and devices. This means that colour is handled on every piece of your equipment, from computer monitor to desktop printer, in exactly the same way. To achieve this, you must calibrate your monitor to ensure it is properly set for colour balance and brightness. From this calibration process, a Colour Profile is created that can be used by image editing packages, such as Photoshop. Calibration should be carried out as often as once a week to ensure it remains consistent.

The calibration process

The screen calibration process varies depending on your computer, but they're all broadly similar. I use an Apple Mac, and calibrate its screen through Apple's ColorSync Utility. Once you have found your computer's screen controls in System Preferences or the Settings folder on your hard drive, you can start using the Screen Calibration Wizard that walks you though the necessary steps.

First, select a 'Target Gamma', which is a basic contrast adjustment: Mac Gamma is 1.8; for a PC,

2.2 is the norm. Next, you determine the screen's 'Native Response', or its luminance properties. A series of sliders and striped images appears, which have to be adjusted until you're happy.

Now, select the 'White Point', which is, basically, the colour temperature of the display. The 'Native' setting will be very blue-white but for imaging you will need to use a setting of around 5000k, a similar colour to white paper viewed under normal daylight. This will look quite warm at first but your eyes will quickly adjust. Finally, save the settings.

You can also calibrate using a Monitor Spyder. These devices are attached to the monitor and measure its colour output, helping to create extremely accurate colour profiles. Primarily used by professionals, Spyders are expensive but may be worth investigating.

Calibrating your monitor

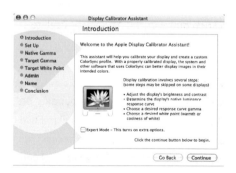

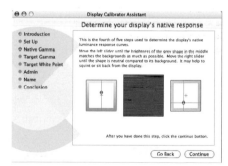

The start screen for calibrating the monitor on an Apple Mac looks like this. By following the prompts, you can calibrate your monitor correctly. What you see on screen should match any printed output. Carry out the calibration process at the time of day you'll be using the screen, as the calibration will vary according to the light levels in your room.

This display gives you an idea of the sliders you will encounter in the screen calibration Wizard. These allow you to fine-tune the screen's response to colour and brightness. It is a good idea to sit further back from the screen and squint during this part of the process, as it helps you achieve the correct brightness and neutrality.

Downloading, storage and back-up

You will need to transfer your shots onto a computer and, for additional security, save them to a separate back-up in case your computer crashes at a later date, losing all your images.

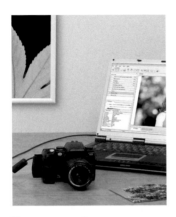

You can connect your camera directly to the computer via a USB or FireWire connection and download your images. This will save you having to use a separate memory card reader.

Connecting the camera

Your DSLR will come with a variety of cables, some of which enable you to connect the camera directly to your computer. The cable, whether a USB or FireWire (you may have a camera with both), allows you to offload your images to your computer for safe storage and image manipulation. You can also transfer data from a memory card with a memory card reader; they're fast, easy to use and save on battery power.

Depending on whether your camera has a USB or FireWire connection or both, you'll be able to plug the camera into a spare USB or FireWire port (it doesn't matter which you use). Computers with USB 2.0 or FireWire connections will be faster than the older USB 1.0 types. To connect, plug one end of the lead you're going to use into the relevant port on your camera, then plug the other end into a spare (and relevant) port on your computer.

Turn your camera on and it will automatically 'see' the computer and 'talk' to it; on some cameras, you have to activate the playback mode (press the review button) to get them talking. The camera should mount as a small hard drive icon on the desktop from which you can drag and drop your images to a folder. Depending on how your computer is set up, it may offload the images to a designated 'Pictures' folder automatically or you may have to create a folder first.

Memory card readers

These small devices are designed to accept a variety of memory cards which can be left plugged into a spare port on your computer; there is no need for extra software to use them. As the memory card reader is plugged into the computer, not the camera, you save camera battery power, and a reader is often faster in terms of shifting image data. To use one is simplicity itself: just plug the memory card into the slot on the card reader that corresponds to it. The card is then mounted on the desktop.

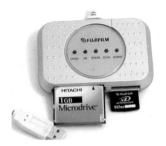

This card reader is designed to accept multiple memory cards of varying types. Use to transfer images from the camera's memory cards onto your computer.

Wireless connection

Transferring your images by wireless connectivity, which allows any WiFi device or camera to connect seamlessly with another WiFi-enabled device, is now becoming an increasingly common practice. An obvious advantage of WiFi is that it cuts down on the cable clutter that quickly builds up on your desk and it allows you to beam images to your computer from anywhere within range of the WiFi system that you are using. Bluetooth is another wireless connection type; it has a shorter connection range than WiFi devices but it works in broadly the same way, although it is slower.

Storage and organization

Your saved images will quickly fill up the hard drive, and you will need to start thinking about organizing and storing them. There are external hard drives available for this, ranging from a few gigabytes up to many hundreds, even thousands. They are very simple to use and set up, plugging straight into your computer via a spare USB or FireWire port.

must know

Some image editing packages come with organizing abilities. These can provide a way to browse your entire library as thumbnails, sorting the images by date, for example, as well as putting them on the web.

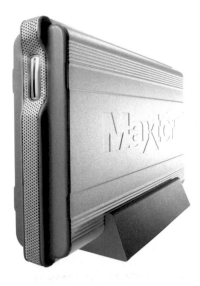

An external hard drive connects to your computer quickly and easily, providing extra storage space – ideal for backing-up important data, such as images.

must know

Whatever method you choose, make sure that back-ups occur regularly and try to keep your data as organized as you can on your computer. It saves time when looking for the data to back up, which is particularly important if you are doing the job manually.

Backing-up

If you keep all your images on just one computer and there is a problem with it, you risk losing them. That's where backing-up comes in. You just move or copy your important data to a different location, whether another computer, an external hard drive or even CDs or DVDs. Helpfully, many external hard drives provide software as part of the package when you buy them for just this purpose.

Some computer operating systems have back-up systems built into them. Windows XP Home Edition is one such system, although the back-up is not installed by default and must be installed from the supplied disks. The most common back-up method, though, is a scheduled back-up to an external hard drive. Back-ups should always be made on a regular basis, determined by how much data you can lose comfortably should something go wrong. You can schedule automatic back-ups on a daily, weekly or monthly basis. The more data is changed or added, the more frequently back-ups should be carried out.

You don't need software to carry out back-ups – you could just copy or move data from its location on your computer to an external hard drive, but you must remember to do it, and do it regularly. You can back up to a CD or DVD if you have a disk writer. However, with CDs holding only 700MB of data each, DVDs are more practical options: single density disks hold 4.7GB, while double density disks hold up to 8GB. Even so, you may need more than one disk and you'll need to swap disks as they become full. If it's at all likely that you'll forget to do a regular manual back-up, you'd be best off using software that does it for you automatically.

Processing RAW files

Shooting images with the RAW capture setting on your DSLR camera provides an indispensable extra level of image control, thereby allowing you to revamp a photograph completely, if you so wish, on your computer at a later date.

Advantages of shooting RAW

You have shot all your images, downloaded the RAW files, and now you are ready to sort through them to choose those that you want to process. As RAW images don't undergo any processing in camera, unlike JPEGs, which have compression and other parameters applied, depending on how the camera is set, RAW images can be thought of as digital versions of film negatives – they contain the raw image data before you have gone into the darkroom (or, in this case, the computer) to get the final print.

The key advantage of working with RAW images is that you can process them later on a computer, adjusting almost every aspect of them, if necessary, including colour saturation, exposure, sharpness and brightness, and even making allowances for vignetting characteristics of your lens.

Manipulating RAW files in Photoshop

Although the following information (see pages 170–171) and accompanying computer images relate to Photoshop, bear in mind that most other image manipulation software, whether it's provided by the camera manufacturers or by third-party developers, operates along similar lines.

must know

If you have many similar images all shot at the same time in identical conditions, you can apply the same processing parameters to multiple images using the Previous Conversion command in the drop-down menu of the right-hand Settings panel. Some software may enable you to batch-process whole folders of images without feeding them in one at a time.

Editing a RAW image

1 Open your folder of images in the software, such as Photoshop. This will load all the images in the folder for you to peruse and select those you want to process.

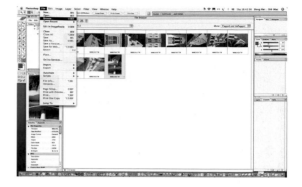

2 Double-click on the image you wish to edit – it will open in a new window. Depending on the image, the software may apply corrections automatically, which can sometimes be enough to rectify the image. But if you feel additional elements need some tweaking, you can then make corrections yourself.

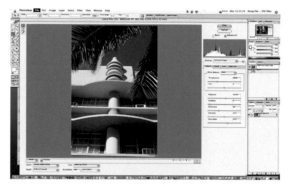

3 Use the sliders to make any necessary changes: adjusting White Balance, increasing Exposure to produce a high-key image, changing Saturation to boost colours. The changes you make cannot damage your RAW file, so you can be more extreme than with a JPEG. The eyedropper tool will fine-tune the white, grey and black points of your image.

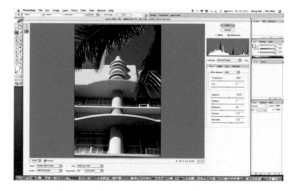

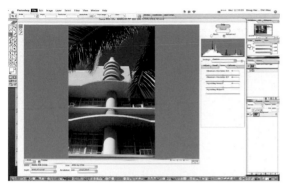

4 Change other settings, such as sharpness, lens vignetting adjustments, individual colour saturation and hue, using the additional tabs in the stacked control panel. Click the relevant tab and make the changes. Click on the preview button to ensure any changes are displayed on screen; if you don't like a certain effect, you can easily change it.

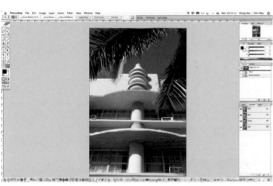

5 When you're happy with your changes (you can see some of the adjustments made to this image on the control panel sliders), click OK for the software to apply your changes and process the file for further editing, if needed, or you can simply save it ready for printing.

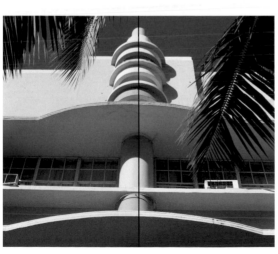

6 This side-by-side comparison shows how the adjustments have improved the RAW image. On the left of the black line you can see the unadjusted RAW file; on the right is the finished, processed image ready to print. The colour overall is much brighter and more vibrant, and the contrast is greatly improved.

Fine-tuning your images

Once you've processed your RAW images and saved them to your computer's hard drive, you are ready to start playing with those images that could be improved with just a little bit more work.

The quick fix

Although your processed images might be almost exactly as you'd like them, there may be tweaks to colour, contrast and sharpness you can make, or you may spot an element that you want to remove. With software such as Photoshop CS (used here) and similar packages (dialogues and menus may vary but the processes are basically the same), you can adjust all these elements on your computer before printing and putting your images into a folio.

Most image editing software has a Quick Fix mode, allowing the software to make a 'best guess' attempt at fixing 'problems' in a shot. Illustrated below is the Quick Fix window for Adobe Photoshop Elements III with before and after examples of the changes made. The Quick Fix mode may save time but its effect can be too much; that's where the next tools come in.

Compare the original image on the left of the screen grab with the one on the right, which has been altered in Quick Fix mode. Quick Fix has automatically adjusted the contrast and colour, making the image more vibrant and boosting brightness.

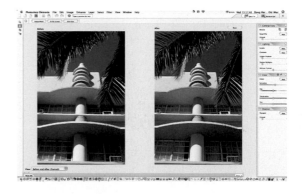

Levels

The Levels adjustment helps control colour and brightness within an image and it allows you to change all the colours or individual ones easily and quickly. The histogram in Levels shows at a glance the quality of the image. This is a graph of all the coloured pixels (and their relative brightness) within the image. A well-exposed image will appear with gentle peaks across the entire histogram. If the histogram shows that the pixels do not reach both ends of the graph (darker pixels are represented on the left, brighter pixels to the right), you can make adjustments.

Adjusting Levels

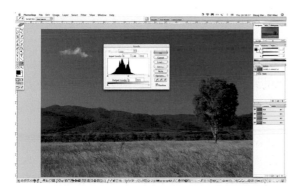

1 Open the image and navigate to Image > Adjustments > Levels. Assess the histogram in the Levels dialogue box for any beneficial adjustments. The pixels in this histogram don't reach both ends of the graph and the Levels could be adjusted to improve the image. Click on the Preview box to see the effect of your adjustments.

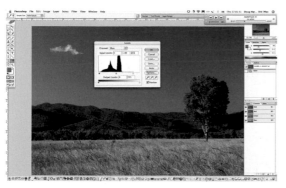

2 Click the Channel drop-down menu and select Red. Move the small pointers beneath the histogram and monitor the effect your changes have on the image as you go. Repeat the process with Green and Blue or until you get the desired result.

Curves

The Curves command is similar to Levels but gives finer control over tones and brightness within an image. Careful control of curves makes it possible to fine-tune colour balance without affecting another part of the image. It's ideal for images containing fine detail, such as clouds or a bride's white dress.

Adjusting Curves

1 Open the image to be edited. Navigate to Image > Adjustment > Curves. The diagonal line in the Curves dialogue box shows the tones within the images and runs from bottom left (the blackest parts of the image) to top right (the whitest parts) through the central area (the grey areas).

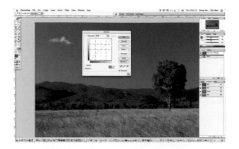

2 Go to the drop-down menu Channels, which allows you to alter each of the three red, green and blue colours independently of each other for fine control. Alternatively, you can adjust them together in the combined, or global, RGB channel. Clicking and dragging on the diagonal line makes the adjustments.

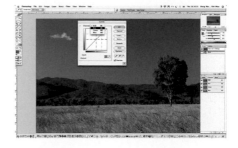

3 Select three anchor points: one in the middle of the dialogue box, one midway between the centre and top, and one midway between the centre and bottom. An 'S' curve usually works best. Drag the top and bottom points in each colour in turn (or globally) until you have the desired degree of adjustment. Then save your image. As with Levels, you can save any settings for use on similar images.

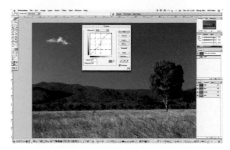

Contact sheets

A contact sheet is a term from the days of film, whereby you create a single sheet of thumbnail-size images of your negatives for editing before printing. In a digital darkroom with software like Photoshop, which uses a system called Contact Sheet II, you can quickly create a contact sheet of your images.

Creating a contact sheet

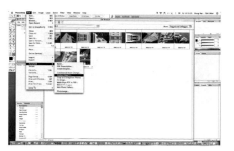

1 Navigate to the folder of images from where you want to create a contact sheet using File > Automate > Contact sheet. A dialogue box will appear in which you decide how you want your contact sheet to look. Your instructions are carried out automatically.

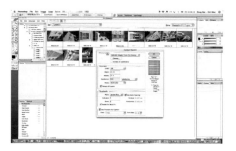

2 Select from the drop-down menu whether you want to make a contact sheet from a folder of images or from the images in the browser window, as shown. Set the document size, using the fields in the dialogue box, set the size of each thumbnail, output resolution, colour mode, etc. Use the image file names as captions or set your own. Use the preview to see how the contact sheet might look.

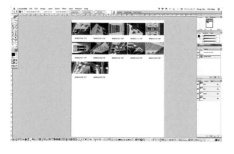

3 Click OK when satisfied that you've set everything properly. The software will start to churn through the data, building your contact sheet automatically as it goes. Once you have a finished contact sheet, as shown here, save it to your hard drive, ready for printing.

Printing

Printing your images is one of the last tasks to perform once you have completed your edits and RAW file processing. There are some key considerations to bear in mind, as well as different ways in which to have your images printed.

Printing options

Your photographs can be printed in a variety of ways – at home on a desktop printer, online or at a high street developers. However, as the quality of your prints is probably of prime importance, you will need to determine the kind of paper and ink that are used by each processor.

Printing at home

This image shows a Canon inkjet printer, typical of the thermal inkjet type of printer.

There are two main types of inkjet printer: thermal and piezo ejection. Thermal inkjets use heat to fire tiny droplets of ink out of nozzles, controlled by the printer and/or your computer. Piezo ejection is different in that it uses minuscule mechanical pumps (one for each nozzle) to eject droplets of ink

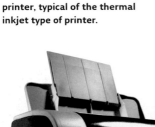

(again controlled by the printer and/or computer) onto the paper. Both types of inkjet, which are becoming more inexpensive to buy, can produce amazing quality prints from their respective photo-output modes. Printer inks are designed to work with specifically designed paper or media. Use media designed for your printer and ink type, so you have the correct colour performance and are guaranteed the best results for the longest amount of time.

Speciality papers, such as fibre-based media and canvas media, are available for more professional or traditional photographic effects, and are useful if you plan to exhibit your pictures. Typically, these papers are made by third-party manufacturers and available in light- or heavyweight versions with a variety of finishes. While the finishes are very good, products are available, such as Print Guard, that can seal the image from the environment and fingermarks and give the print a lift into the bargain.

must know

Just like taking a roll of film in to be processed, you can now go into a print shop, hand over your memory card or a CD of images you've prepared at home and have prints made. Some of these shops will also have do-it-yourself print kiosks, so you can print out your own images via a touch screen.

Printing online

Online printing necessitates a connection to the internet. Ideally, that connection should be fast because image files can be very large and take a long time to upload. You can upload your images to a number of online organizations (see page 189), who store the images in folders or online albums, print them for you to your requirements and then post them back. You can even get CDs of the images as well.

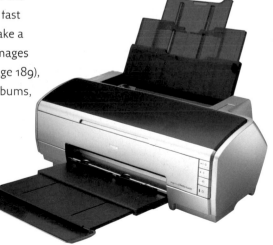

Epson inkjet printers, like the printer illustrated here, use piezo ejection technology.

Black-and-white from colour

Not all DSLRs allow you to shoot in black-and-white mode and even if your DSLR camera does, it's best to shoot in colour because you then have the option of creating black-and-white images on the computer.

Desaturation and greyscale

The easiest way to convert a colour image into black-and-white is to desaturate it by navigating to Image > Adjustments > Desaturate, as shown below. This is, however, a particularly crude method and the image will end up looking flat, especially in the highlights and shadows. I would use this method only to give me a quick idea of what a colour image might look like in black-and-white. An alternative method is to convert the colour image to greyscale. To do this, go to Image > Mode > Greyscale. This method has its limitations, too, and it is 'destructive' in the sense that it changes the image file permanently.

Using desaturation

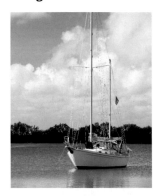

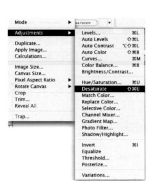

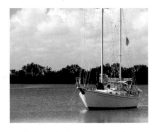

1 Open the colour image in Photoshop or chosen software.

2 Navigate to Image > Adjustments > Desaturate.

3 Although the converted image looks acceptable, there are better ways of doing the job, giving you more control over the way in which the different tones are displayed.

Hue/Saturation method

Converting a colour image to black-and-white using the Hue/Saturation method and adjusting the Hue, Saturation and Lightness can produce a wide range of different effects. There are no hard-and-fast rules regarding the 'perfect' version. Of the three images below, it is the last that works best for me, and it is certainly a great improvement over the simple desaturate version shown opposite.

Using Hue/Saturation

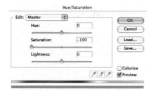

2 Change the second new layer from Normal to Color in the Layers palette in the drop-down window. In the Hue/Saturation box, click Colorize. Move the sliders (Hue, Saturation and Lightness) to different positions to create the desired tonal effect. Three different variations are shown below.

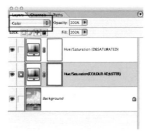

1 Navigate to Layer > New Adjustment Layer > Hue/Saturation and create two new layers. For the top layer, move the Saturation slider to -100 to turn off the colour.

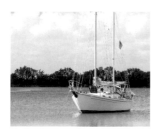
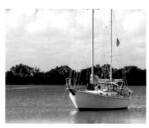
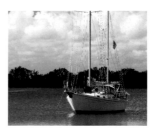

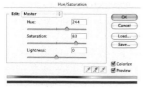
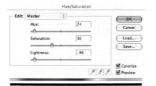
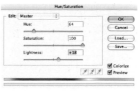

Channel mixer

My preferred method of changing a colour image to black-and-white is to use the Channel mixer. Increasing or decreasing the values of the red, green and blue channels can produce very similar effects to using colour filters with black-and-white film.

Using Channel mixer

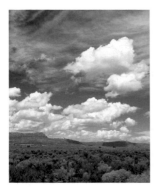

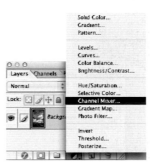

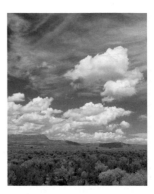

1 Start off by opening the colour image in Photoshop or the equivalent software on your computer.

2 Click on the middle icon at the bottom of the Layers palette, as highlighted here. Select Channel Mixer.

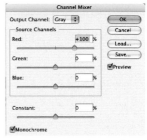

3 Tick the Monochrome box in the Channel Mixer box (above) to remove the colour from the image (top).

must know

Remember that if you do decide to shoot in black-and-white, you will not be able to convert to colour later on.

Red filter mode

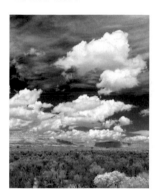

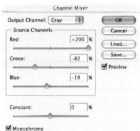

Green filter mode

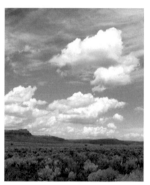

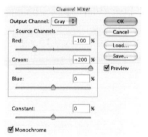

Yellow filter mode

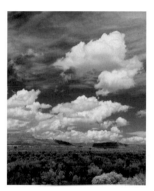

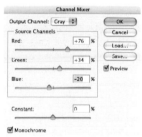

4 Move the sliders to achieve the desired effect – here, it is to emulate a red filter, darkening the sky and enhancing clouds. Keep a full range of tones by making the sum of the values close to 100, as shown here (+200 Red / -82 Green / -18 Blue = 100). Tick the Preview box to monitor your changes.

5 Emulating a green filter by increasing the value in the Green channel has flattened and lightened the foliage in the shot. Remember that using a filter the same colour as the subject will have the effect of lightening it, whereas using a complementary one will darken it.

6 Emulating a yellow filter results in less drastic changes. The sky has darkened but not as much as with the red filter. However, there is much more detail in the cloud. In my opinion, this is the best version because it displays a full range of tones and will make a first-rate black-and-white print.

Presenting your images

Once you've successfully edited and perhaps even printed your images, you may want to share them with others. There are so many great ways to present your images to the world.

Choosing your presentation

There are many ways of presenting your work, and you may need a combination of them, from a printed portfolio to your own website. How you present your images depends on how they will be used. Be strict and edit them rigorously, then edit them again to include only the best pictures. Update your folio on a regular basis, particularly if you're aiming to sell your images – a folio of images for one prospective client might not be at all suitable for another.

Traditional folios

In a printed portfolio, you need the highest-quality images. Desktop printers are ideal for this, as you can quickly update the folio as well as achieving high-quality prints from material and originals that you can control. Folios can be expensive but make a good first impression. Buy a folio of archival quality, made from materials that won't leach chemicals into your prints, skew colours or make the prints fade. It should be sufficiently robust to carry around as well as protecting your work and presenting it to the best advantage.

A good-quality folio containing your best images is an effective presentation tool, particularly if you're touting for business or intending to sell your images.

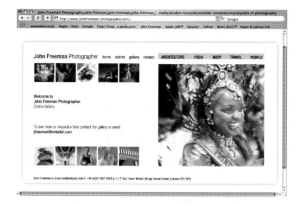

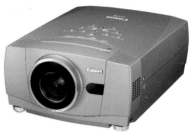

A website can be expensive to build, but most image-editing software has quick, easy-to-use tools to help you build a basic online folio of images.

A digital projector is an ideal way to present your images if they've been burnt onto a DVD.

Web presentation

Building a modest website to present your images is a good idea, allowing you to get them online quickly and efficiently for prospective clients. Many image-editing programs come with simple-to-use web-building elements to help you create a website. A bespoke web build can be expensive, so consider free online sharing communities (see page 189).

Folios on disk

Another route is to burn a slide show of your images onto a DVD or CD. There are numerous film-making software packages available with your computer's operating system, such as iMovie, for creating professional-looking slide shows. You can present these on your computer or project them with a digital projector. If you have lots of large images, use a DVD, not a CD, because it has a capacity of 4.7GB as opposed to 700MB. Projectors can be plugged into a computer, which can be used to control the show, or into a DVD player with a disk with a pre-burnt slide show presentation on board.

want to know more?

• Specialist photography magazines feature the latest equipment news.
• Look at consumables websites to compare prices of computer kit, e.g. external hard drives.
• The following websites all contain some useful information. Log on to:
www.adobe.com
www.apple.com
www.epson.co.uk
www.canon.co.uk

Glossary

Alpha channel
Extra 8-bit greyscale channel in an image that is used for creating masks to isolate part of the image.

Angle finder
Device attached to a viewfinder allowing an image to be viewed at right angles to the camera.

Aperture
Variable opening in the lens that determines how much light is allowed to pass through the lens.

Aperture priority
Camera metering mode that allows you to select the aperture, while the camera automatically selects the shutter speed.

APO (Apochromatic) lens
Lens that reduces flare and gives greater accuracy in colour rendition.

ASA (American Standards Association)
Series of numbers that denotes the speed of camera film, now superseded by the ISO number, which is identical.

Auto-focus
Lens that focuses automatically on the chosen subject.

AWB (Automatic White Balance)
Automatic assessment by the camera of white balance.

B (bulb setting)
Setting on the shutter speed dial on the camera that keeps the shutter open for as long as the shutter release is pressed.

Backlight
Light behind your subject, falling onto the front of the camera.

Barn doors
Movable pieces of metal that are attached to the front of a studio light to flag unwanted light.

Beauty dish
White dish within a reflective baffle that reflects light onto the subject with a very even spread of light, similar to a satellite dish.

Between the lens shutter
Shutter built into the lens that allows flash synchronization at all shutter speeds.

Bit
Unit of computer information.

Boom
Attachment for a studio light that allows the light to be suspended at a variable distance from the studio stand.

Bracketing
Method of exposing one or more frames either side of the predicted exposure and at slightly different exposures.

Byte
Computer file size measurement:
1024 bits = 1 byte,
1024 bytes = 1 kilobyte,
1024 kilobytes = 1 megabyte,
1024 megabytes = 1 gigbyte.

Cable release
Attachment that allows for the smooth operation of the shutter.

Calibration
Means of adjusting screen, scanner, etc. for accurate colour output.

CCD (Charge Coupled Device)
Light sensor.

CD R
Recordable CD.

CD RW
Recordable CD that can be overwritten.

CdS
Cadmium sulphide cell used in electronic exposure meters.

Centre-weighted metering
TTL metering system that is biased towards the centre of the frame.

CMYK
Cyan, magenta, yellow colour printing method used in inkjet printers.

Colour bit depth
Number of bits that are used to represent each pixel that makes up an image.

Colour temperature
Scale for measuring the colour temperature of light in Kelvins (K). 5000K is the colour temperature of daylight.

Compact flash card
Removable storage media used in digital cameras. Also known as a memory card.

Compression
Various methods used to reduce the size of a file. Often achieved by removing colour data (see JPEG).

Continuous auto-focus
Method whereby a camera

focuses automatically, even when the subject is moving.

Continuous lighting
Flicker-free source of light balanced to daylight. Also known as HMI.

Contrast
Range of tones in an image.

Cyan
Blue-green light whose complementary colour is red.

Data
Information used in computing.

Dedicated flash
Method by which the camera assesses the amount of light that is required and adjusts the flash output accordingly.

Default
Standard setting for a command or software tool if the settings have not been changed by the operator.

Depth of field
Distance in front of the point of focus and the distance beyond that is acceptably sharp.

Dialogue box
Window in a computer application like Photoshop where the user can change the settings.

Diaphragm
Adjustable blades in the lens that determine the size of the aperture.

Diffuser
Material such as tracing paper that is placed over a light source to soften the light.

Digital zoom
Digital camera feature that enlarges central part of the image at the expense of quality.

Download
Transfer of information from one piece of computer equipment to another.

DPI (Dots Per inch)
Measure of resolution of a printed image (see PPI).

Duotone
Black-and-white image that has another colour added later on the computer.

EVF (Electronic viewfinder)
Type of viewfinder found in high-end digital cameras.

Exposure meter
Instrument that measures the amount of light on the subject.

Extender
Device fitting between the camera body and lens that increases the focal length of the lens.

Extension bellows
Attachment that enables the lens to focus at a closer distance than normal.

Extension tube
Attachment that fits between the camera and the lens to allow close-up photography.

F/number
Aperture setting of the lens. Also known as f/stop.

File format
Method of storing information in a file, such as JPEG and TIFF.

Filter
Device fitted over or behind the camera lens to correct or enhance the final photograph.

Filter factor
Amount of exposure increase required to compensate for a particular filter.

Firewire™
High-speed data transfer device up to 800 mbps (megabits per second). Also known as IEEE 1394.

Fisheye lens
Lens with an angle of view of 180°.

Fixed focus
Lens whose focusing cannot be adjusted.

Flag
Piece of material to stop light spill.

Flare
Effect of unwanted light entering the lens and ruining the shot.

Flash memory
Fast memory chip that retains all its data even when the power is switched off.

Focal plane shutter
Shutter system that uses blinds close to the focal plane.

Focusing screen
Area that the eye focuses on when looking through the viewfinder.

Fringe
Unwanted border of extra pixels around a selection caused by lack of a hard edge.

Gel
Coloured material that can be placed over lights either for an effect or to colour correct or balance.

Ghosting
Hexagonal shapes caused by surface reflections in front of the aperture.

GIF (Graphic Interchange Format)
Compressed file format used over the internet.

Gigabyte
One billion bytes.

Gobo
Device used in a spotlight to create different patterns of light.

Golden section
Theory used by artists to give a pleasing composition. Also known as rule of thirds.

Glossary

Greyscale
Image that comprises 256 shades of grey.

Hard drive
Internal permanent storage system of a computer.

High key
Photographs where most of the tones are taken from the light end of the scale.

Histogram
Graphical representation of variables over a range of values.

HMI
See Continuous lighting.

Honeycomb
Device fitted to the front of a light source that creates a directional light.

Honeycomb metering
See Matrix metering.

Hotshoe
Device that is usually mounted on the top of the camera, for attaching accessories, such as flash.

Image stabilization
Method for reducing camera shake especially when using a telephoto lens.

Incident light reading
Method of reading the exposure required by measuring the light falling on the subject.

Internal storage
Built-in memory found in some digital cameras.

Interpolation
Increasing the number of pixels in an image.

Invercone
Attachment placed over the exposure meter for taking incident light readings.

ISO (International Standards Organization)
Rating used for film speed that has been replicated in digital photography denoting sensitivity.

JPEG (Joint Photographic Expert Group)
File format for storing digital photographs in which the original image is compressed to just a fraction of its original size.

Kelvin (κ)
Unit of measurement of colour temperature.

LCD (Liquid Crystal Display)
Flat-screen display of information.

Lens hood
Device fitted to the front of the lens for shielding it from extraneous light.

Lens shield
Performs the same function as a lens hood but is generally attached to the camera lens with a flexible arm.

Lossless
File compression that does not lose any data or quality.

Lossy
File compression that does lose some data.

Low key
Photographs where most of the tones are taken from the dark end of the scale.

Macro lens
Lens that enables you to take close-up photographs.

Magenta
Complementary colour to green, formed by a mixture of red and blue light.

Matrix metering
Method of customizing the camera's colour space. Also known as multi-zone or honeycomb metering.

Megabyte
One million bytes.

Megapixel
1,000,000 pixels.

Memory card
See Compact flash card.

Mirror lock
Device on some DSLR cameras that allows you to lock the mirror up before taking your shot in order to minimize vibration.

Moiré
Interference pattern similar to the clouded appearance of watered silk.

Monobloc
Flash unit with the power pack built into the head.

Montage
Image formed from combining a number of different photographs.

Multi-zone metering
See Matrix metering

Network
Group of computers linked by cables or a wireless system so they can share files. The web is a huge network.

Neutral density filter
Filter that can be placed over the lens or light source to reduce the required exposure.

Noise
Grainy effect in images occurring in low light.

Pan tilt head
Accessory placed on the top of a tripod that allows smooth camera movements in a variety of directions.

Panning
Method of moving the camera in line with a fast-moving subject in order to create the feeling of speed.

PC lens
Perspective control, or shift, lens.

Photoshop
Image manipulation software package (industry standard).
Pixel
The element from which a digitized image is made up.
Polarizing filter
Filter that darkens blue skies and cuts out unwanted reflections.
PPI (Pixels Per Inch)
Measure of resolution of an image (see DPI).
Predictive focus
Mode of focusing whereby the lens memorizes a selected point of focus while focusing on another subject.
Prime lens
Lens with a fixed focal length, unlike a zoom lens.
RAM (Random Access Memory)
Component of a computer in which information can be stored temporarily and accessed quickly.
RAW
The digital equivalent of a film negative.
Resolution
Measure of the amount of pixels in an image.
RGB (Red, Green and Blue)
Colour model used to represent the colour spectrum.
Ring flash
Flash unit where the tube fits around the lens, giving almost shadowless lighting.
Satellite dish
Similar to a beauty dish.

Shift and tilt lens
Lens that allows you to shift its axis to control perspective and tilt to control the plane of sharp focus.
Shutter
Means of controlling amount of time that light is allowed to pass through the lens.
Shutter lag
Delay between pressing the shutter release and the picture being taken.
Shutter priority
Metering system in the camera that allows the photographer to set the shutter speed while the camera sets the aperture automatically.
Single area auto-focus
Mode of focusing that finds the main subject in a scene.
Slave unit
Device for synchronizing one flash unit to another.
Snoot
Lighting attachment that enables a beam of light to be concentrated in a small circle.
Soft box
Attachment placed on the front of a light, giving diffused illumination.
Spill
Lighting attachment for controlling the spread of light.
Spot metering
Method of exposure meter reading over a very small area.
Stop
Aperture setting on a lens.

Studio flash
Powerful form of flash light.
Terabyte
One trillion bytes.
Tele converter
Device that fits between the camera and lens to extend the focal length of the lens.
TIFF (Tagged Inventory File Format)
Format for storing digital images.
TTL (Through The Lens)
Exposure metering system.
Umbrella
Umbrella-shaped attachment that reflects light from a studio flash head.
USB (Universal Serial Bus)
Industry standard connector for attaching peripheral devices, such as a digital camera, to a computer, with data transfer rates of up to 450mbps (megabits per second).
Vignetting
Darkening of the corners of the frame if a device, e.g. a filter, is used that is too small for the angle of view of the lens.
White balance
Method used for accurately recording the correct colours in different light sources.
Zip
External storage device that accepts cartridges between 100 and 750 megabytes.
Zoom lens
Lens with a variable focal length.

Need to know more?

Manufacturers

This is a selection of leading manufacturers of digital cameras, lenses and accessories.

www.canon.co.uk
www.fujifilm.co.uk
www.nikon.co.uk
www.olympus.co.uk
www.pentax.co.uk
www.sony.co.uk

Flash

Metz is the market leader for on-camera flashguns, while Johnsons-photopia (Broncolor) and Elinchrom are popular makes of professional studio flash kit.

www.elinchrom.com
www.johnsons-photopia.co.uk
www.metzflash.co.uk

Reflectors

You can use a range of materials to improvise a reflector, such as white card or a sheet. For a huge range of proprietary ones, try Lastolite.

www.lastolite.com

Equipment retailers

Some professional retailers also rent out equipment. This means that that you can try before you buy, possibly saving you money in the long run.

www.calumetphoto.co.uk
www.jessops-uk.co.uk
www.jigsaw24.com
www.robertwhite.co.uk
www.teamworkphoto.com

Distributors and importers

These distributors cover a wide range of popular and lesser-known items of kit.

www.intro2020.co.uk
www.johnsons-photopia.co.uk

Printers

Canon is the market leader for inkjet printers but the others are catching up fast.

www.canon.co.uk
www.epson.co.uk
www.hp.co.uk

Fine art inkjet papers

Every month new printing papers are marketed. As well as the usual finishes, such as glossy or matt, many have textured surfaces.

www.chaudigital.com (Da Vinci)
www.epson.co.uk
www.fotospeed.com
www.hahnemuehle.com
www.inveresk.co.uk (Somerset)
www.permajet.com

Online printing

You can upload your image files to various organizations who will store and print your images.
www.bonusprint.co.uk (one of many traditional photo printing companies that now work online)
www.foto.com
www.metroimaging.co.uk
www.photobox.co.uk
www.snapfish.co.uk

Professional digital printers

These printing companies produce work to the highest standard.
www.johnfreeman-photographer.com
www.metroimaging.co.uk
www.tapestry.co.uk

Sensor cleaning and repair

Although there are many kits on the market, I would recommend that you have your sensor cleaned professionally by a company such as Fixation.
www.fixationuk.com

Web presentation

The following sites are free online sharing communities, where you can upload your images to be accessed by interested parties.
www.flickr.com
Google Images
www.myspace.com

Galleries and organizations

These organizations are a good resource centre for students and assistants.
www.michaelhoppengallery.com
www.photofusion.org
www.photonet.org.uk (The Photographers' Gallery)
www.tate.org.uk/modern (Tate Modern)
www.the-aop.org (The Association of Photographers)
www.vam.ac.uk/collections/photography (Victoria & Albert Museum)

Bibliography

Adobe Photoshop Elements 5.0 A-Z
Andrews, Philip, *Tools and Features Illustrated Ready Reference*
Evening, Martin, *Adobe Photoshop for Photographers*

Magazines

Digital Photographer
www.dphotographer.co.uk
The British Journal of Photography
www.bjphoto.co.uk
Digital Camera
www.dcmag.co.uk
Mac Format
www.macformat.co.uk
PC Format
www.pcformat.co.uk

Index

The author

John Freeman is a highly experienced professional photographer and author of many books on photography, including *Practical Photography*, *Lighting for Interiors and Photography: The Complete Guide to Taking Photographs*. He has a regular column in *What Digital Camera?* and *Digital Camera magazines*. For further information and a gallery of his photographs, visit www.johnfreeman-photographer.com.

Acknowledgements

I would like to thank the following organizations for their help in the preparation of this book: Adobe Photoshop; Apple Computers; Calumet UK; Canon Cameras UK; Epson Printers; Fast Track UK; Intro 2020; Fujifilm UK; Kodak; MotorSport Vision Ltd; Nikon Cameras UK; Olympus Cameras UK; Sigma Imaging UK; Sony UK; The Hop Shop, Shoreham, Kent; Phlox Flowers, London.

This book would not have been possible without my team of assistants: Alex Dow, my digital guru, who has been there for eight previous books and is indispensable; David Horwich, Jamie Laing, Simon Lipman, James Meakin, Ade Saul Osoba and Joas Souza, all of whom are destined to become great photographers!

John Freeman